"Bethany is an amazing young woman who loves people the way Jesus said he wanted us to. The way she lives her life is as unconventional as Jesus's life. You'll enjoy
love and what's she's learning abou
of the people around her."

"Bethany's long obedience in the st
dearing and inspiring. Raw, witty, and unafraid, *One Dress. One Year.* is a primer on moving from passion to action. This book is a must-read for any person who is passionate about justice but unsure of where to begin—or if their efforts will even matter."

Jim Martin, vice president of spiritual formation, International Justice Mission, author of *The Just Church*

"As much as the world needs people with a passion for freedom, it may need the other gift Bethany Winz offers here even more: vulnerability and a heart that is open to God and others. Bethany is part of a brave new generation of leaders who follow Jesus as they engage with some of the world's most difficult issues—and most vulnerable people. I encourage you to listen to her creative and courageous voice inviting others on a journey to freedom!"

Jennifer Roemhildt Tunehag, cofounder and core team member, Human Trafficking Task Force, World Evangelical Alliance

"They say, 'Clothes make a person.' Really? How about the same dress worn forever . . . or for a whole year? I'm not sure that clothes make a person, but Bethany allowed a single dress to talk for her. And what a single dress said over and over and over and over was . . . *humans matter*. This book will introduce you to a real person who cares. Listen to her dress. It has a lot to say."

Dan Boone, president, Trevecca Nazarene University

"Love is God's call to us: demonstrating compassion and passion for those in need, speaking out and taking action, giving generously and sacrificially. All of these evidences of God's love flow from Bethany Winz in her commitment to address the abomination of human slavery in a simple but sacrificial choice: to wear one dress for one year. You will love her strong voice and gentle spirit, her honesty and humor, as well as her perseverance."

Judy Douglass, writer, speaker, encourager Women's Resources, Cru

One Dress. One Year.

One Girl's Stand
against
Human Trafficking

Bethany Winz WITH
Susanna Foth Aughtmon

BakerBooks
a division of Baker Publishing Group
Grand Rapids, Michigan

Published by Baker Books
a division of Baker Publishing Group
P.O. Box 6287, Grand Rapids, MI 49516-6287
www.bakerbooks.com

Printed in the United States of America

Library of Congress Cataloging-in-Publication Data
Names: Winz, Bethany, 1995– author.
Title: One dress, one year : one girl's stand against human trafficking / Bethany Winz, with Susanna Foth Aughtmon.
Description: Grand Rapids, MI : Baker Books, 2016. | Includes bibliographical references.
Identifiers: LCCN 2015030797 | ISBN 9780801018367
Subjects: LCSH: Winz, Bethany, 1995- | Human trafficking—Prevention—Blogs. | Human trafficking--Religious aspects--Christianity. | Teenage girls—Political activity—United States. | Christian teenagers—Political activity—United States. | Self-realization—Religious aspects—Christianity.
Classification: LCC HQ281 .W566 2016 | DDC 306.3/62—dc23 LC record available at http://lccn.loc.gov/2015030797

Some names and details have been changed to protect the identity of certain individuals.

Published in association with Books & Such Literary Management.

16 17 18 19 20 21 22 7 6 5 4 3 2 1

For Morgan, Erin, Tabitha, and Tori.

This story would have been impossible without you four.

I love you more than you know.

Contents

Acknowledgments

Mom and Dad, thank you so much for your encouragement and support and for not complaining too much when my friends and I lick the counters. It is in the safety of your love that I have found the courage to do the things I've done. I love you more than words can say.

Michael, thanks for being the best big brother a girl could ask for. I'm grateful for the hours we spend talking about everything from theology to school to silly stuff.

Tori, thank you for being a wise, kind, encouraging friend, and for always being up for something crazy. So much of who I am today is because of your friendship. Morgan, Erin, and Tabitha, thanks for the honest conversations and good jokes. I would be lost without you three.

To so many—too many to name here—who came alongside my parents and raised me to know what it means to love and follow Jesus, I am grateful. You've prayed for me, stood with me, and encouraged me. Thank you to my Pine Castle family, and especially to Pastor Sylvia, Mr. Andy, Veronica, Jarrod and Samantha, Mrs. Michelle, Mrs. Kim, Mrs. Mary, Mrs. Sondra, and the Jr. Interns. To my Family Discipleship Ministries family, both named and unnamed in these pages, thank you for your legacy. It is an honor to walk in your footsteps.

Thank you to my many Trevecca friends who have walked with me through college and to the professors who have challenged and encouraged me at every turn. Bree, Emily, and Kat, thank you for being my roommates during the writing process and putting up with me. You're more gracious than I deserve.

Janet, thank you for going after this project and walking me through the process. This book wouldn't exist without you and your patience and encouragement.

Sue, thank you for how hard you worked to pull this together. You helped me find my voice in the midst of this story and figured out how to say things when I couldn't. It's been an honor to work with such a gifted writer.

Rebekah, Nicci, and the rest of the team at Baker, thank you for believing in this book and working to make it a reality.

Thank you to Alex and Brett Harris, Zach Hunter, Elaini, and so many others who helped me believe that I could do more than what was expected of me—even as a teenager. Thank you for your courage. It has given so many of us the courage we needed to take the next step.

To the musicians and writers who have carried me through the past few years, and especially the dark parts, thank you. And many thanks to the writers and teachers who taught me to love words and challenged me to become a better writer.

To all of you who lived this story with me and have allowed me to tell your part in it, thank you. To the countless people who have prayed for me, encouraged me, and helped me get the word out about The Dress Project, thank you. It would not have happened without you. And thank you to the many people who have helped me tell this story by giving feedback on content, grammar, and tone (or by talking me down off a ledge).

And Jesus, thank you for such an amazing year in the dress and all the things you've taught me through this experience. Teach me to steward this story well.

Introduction

> Therefore, as God's chosen people, holy and dearly loved, clothe yourselves with compassion, kindness, humility, gentleness and patience.
>
> Colossians 3:12

When I was in middle school, I found out that slavery still exists. In fact, every morning, millions of men, women, and children around the world wake up trapped in a system of human trafficking. Faced with the same bleak reality day after day, their dreams of freedom remain just that—dreams. I knew it didn't have to be this way, but if anything was going to change, ordinary people, people like you and me, needed to get involved. So at sixteen, I decided to do something about it.

From January 11, 2012, to January 10, 2013, I wore the same black dress every day. It was my way of raising awareness about and money to help end human trafficking across the globe. One Dress. One Year. For Freedom. It was a yearlong journey that I chose. People who are enslaved don't have many choices, so surely

I could limit my clothing choices for a year to help them be free. While my experience wasn't nearly the same thing as what those who are enslaved face, it was a connection I could make to help others understand human trafficking. I then asked people to partner with me by giving to one of six organizations working to end modern-day slavery.

Using the black dress as my primary piece, I added other clothing and accessories to create different looks, and each day I posted a photo of my outfit on my blog. By the end of the year, I'd worn that same black dress in 366 different ways—of course I would pick a leap year. I went into that year thinking I would do something big for God. I was going to raise $100,000 to help end the fight against modern-day slavery. My blog and my dress were going to change the world.

I thought The Dress Project would give me value and make me special. I wanted to prove that I was better than other people my age. After all, unlike many of my peers, I was thinking about *important* things. Sacrificing normal clothes for a year or talking about slavery or challenging others to fight for the same cause was supposed to make me important too. Instead, the year I spent in the dress changed me in ways I never expected. It taught me to pay attention to fashion, and it altered the way I see myself.

That year, the people who partnered with me gave $8,615 to International Justice Mission (IJM), Not for Sale, the A21 Campaign, Compassion International, Restore International, and Love146. The money was used to rescue people, provide them with rehabilitation services and legal counsel, and prevent human trafficking in vulnerable communities.

I'd always been told that pride goes before the fall, but I think some of us fall harder than others. I didn't come anywhere close to my fund-raising goal. Throughout the year I felt like I should have been doing more, but I couldn't figure out what—or how. Nothing seemed to go the way I wanted it to. It didn't make me feel better like I thought it would. Instead, the dress helped me see myself for who I was (and who I still am): a girl who needed to be set free from perfectionism and pride and guilt and the notion that I could buy my way into God's good graces with my grand plans. I couldn't. All I could do was hope that somehow, even when I felt unlovable, he loved me still. The beautiful part was that in my darkness and my doubt, God met me. He's still meeting me. I'm sure your story won't be the same as mine, but I bet if you look closely, you'll find God meeting you too.

The Dress Project was a way that a high school girl helped raise money for organizations that are bringing freedom to people worldwide. During that year, though, I also discovered how much I needed the freedom God can bring. Freedom is for all of us, and it's something all of us can be part of extending to others. But it is only something we can participate in when we know that we are loved, and that we are already free.

—Bethany Winz

1

A Dress and a Dream

The Sewing Factory

A light breeze blows through my cracked bedroom window, causing the blinds to click against one another. Florida nights can be muggy, but in January, the chilly evenings are perfect for sitting on our front porch swing. Of course, for me, any time is perfect for that. Sweltering heat, pouring rain, cool evenings, and even bloodthirsty mosquitoes can't deter me from spending hours swinging back and forth, lost in thought. It's my sanctuary, a safe place to dream. And right now, it's where I want to be. Instead, I'm in my bedroom wrestling with the buttonholes on the front of the black dress I'm sewing. I've been working on this dress for months. A few weeks ago, I finally nailed the design. The entire process has been slow and frustrating, but the buttonholes might be the worst part. These buttons, which are too big for my buttonhole tool, seemed like a good idea when I first started sewing the dress. At that time, the dress itself seemed like a good idea. Now I'm rethinking both.

As I lean forward to thread my Singer sewing machine, a loose curl falls out of my bun and dances at the corner of my eye. Reaching up, I twist it back into the knot of brunette hair at the nape of my neck. I've lived here all of my life, but Florida and my hair have never gotten along. Every day is a new battle to tame my curls.

Once the needle is threaded, I look down at the stack of ten black buttons on my desk and sigh. Lifting the presser foot, I slide the dress off the machine. I stretch over the arm of my chair to grab a piece of scrap material from the floor and then give the buttonholes one more try. It's another flop. While the buttonhole is long enough, it doesn't leave any space for the button to pass through. I push my chair back and stand up. Sewing is not for the faint of heart.

I pace back and forth, trying to take deep breaths. Every time I turn, I see the dress and feel like I might hyperventilate. Tension creeps up my spine and into my shoulders. Flopping down on my bed, I bury my face in my pillow. "This dress is going to kill me," I wail. The dress that's piled on my desk looks nothing like my grand vision, but right now, all I want is to finish it. The plain cotton fabric is exactly what I'd wanted. It's light enough to get me through a Florida summer, and hopefully it will stand up to wash after wash. It hasn't been as no fuss as I'd expected though. The tension moves into my head, and I can feel it pounding in my ears. This year is supposed to be victorious. I'm supposed to be making a statement about how people everywhere can unite to end human trafficking. Right now, though, the only statement I'm making is that I need to take sewing lessons. No matter how hard I try, the perfectionist in me whispers that I can't get anything right—especially not this dress.

I roll over onto my back and stare at the ceiling. Purple and white paint meet in the corner, and I follow the purple down the wall to my bed, which is draped in a bright rainbow-striped quilt. It has every color but purple, so it clashes with the walls. *Maybe I should redecorate my room instead of working on the dress.* The windows, which seem to let in all the heat of summer and all the cool of winter, are curtainless. *I could make some curtains. That would be easier than sewing a dress. Or I could paint the walls. Orange? Yellow? Anything but purple.*

This wouldn't be the first time I started a new project before finishing the last one. A painting project would be more fun than a sewing project. But this isn't just any sewing project. It's supposed to be a sewing project with a purpose. A dress with a mission. This is the dress that I'm going to wear for an entire year to help raise awareness about how pervasive human trafficking has become. This dress is supposed to change the world.

"Dinner's ready," Mom calls from across the house. I pull myself off my bed and shuffle down the hall to the kitchen.

"How's the dress coming?" Dad asks as I walk in. The silverware clinks as he pulls it from the drawer.

I sigh.

"That good, huh?" Michael says, falling into his chair. My big brother is home from college for Christmas break.

"I don't know why I thought buttons this big were a good idea." I slide out the chair diagonal to Michael's and sit down. "I can't figure out how to make the buttonholes work."

"What about the rest of the dress?" Mom puts a plate of steaming barbecue chicken on the table. My mouth waters.

"Well, it doesn't look like a black burlap sack anymore."

She laughs, and I laugh with her. She's seen the dress in every stage of the sewing process. She saw the original pattern that didn't work, and she's seen each step as I've tried to figure it out on my own. Finally, a month ago, I found a design that would work. I thought that I had ironed out all the kinks, but now I'm not so sure.

"I guess that's good," Michael says.

"It doesn't look like the picture in my head, but I think it's going to work."

"I hope it does," Dad says. "Now let's pray."

We bow our heads. Sewing has always been frustrating for me, but I'd hoped that I would be able to master it this time around. Making this dress, however, has been more difficult than I ever imagined it could be. I'm grateful that my family is around to support me. As Dad prays for our food, I start thinking about how I wound up here. A conversation Mom and I had back in September was the beginning of this wild journey.

I've always had more ideas than I've known what to do with. For as long as I can remember, I've been a dreamer. Holding up two fingers to measure the air, Mom used to say, "You're taking something that's this big and turning it into something that's this big," and then she would spread her arms wide. The problem was that I was much better at coming up with ideas than I was at following through with them.

I had a lot of thoughts about how I would like to play a part in ending slavery. That afternoon, she and I sat down and put all my ideas on paper. Should I do a dance production at church to raise awareness about human trafficking or go to the Not for Sale conference? Or should I concentrate on selling the bracelets my friends and I made to raise money for International Justice Mission?

Ever since my best friend, Tori, and I read *Do Hard Things* by Alex and Brett Harris, we've been looking for ways to join what they call The Rebelution: a teenage rebellion against low expectations. People don't seem to expect much from teenagers, but we're convinced that we can have an impact. We want to challenge ourselves and change the world. We've always dreamed ambitious things, but The Rebelution has given us a reason for our dreams. That afternoon with my mom was my plunge into making my Rebelution dreams into a reality.

As Mom and I worked through most of my ideas, I found one more that kept pushing its way forward. I was almost afraid to say it out loud because it seemed so big. It felt impossible. It had to do with Elaini.

Elaini is a young American woman with a huge heart for orphans in India. She couldn't travel overseas but wanted to do something to help them. Many of these children have only one outfit to their name, so for one hundred days she wore just one dress in honor of them. Her mission was to raise $50,000 for an organization working with the children she lovingly calls "her kids." She used accessories to create different outfits and blogged each day, posting pictures of herself in the dress. She also invited her readers to join her in honoring these children by giving money. In just over three months, she exceeded her goal and continued raising money.

"I keep thinking about what it would be like if I did something to end trafficking like what Elaini did to raise money for the orphans."

Mom's eyes got wide.

"But I think I'd want to do it for an entire year like the woman who inspired her."

"You really want to wear the same thing for an entire year?" she asked.

I couldn't stop the words from tumbling out. I explained how I could do it to raise money for International Justice Mission, a global organization that works to end trafficking in the developing world. In the same way that Elaini connected her dress to orphans who had only one set of clothes, I would connect my dress to the plight of those trapped in modern-day slavery. People who are trafficked wake up and face the same thing day after day. I could wake up to the same dress every day. It wouldn't be nearly the same thing, but maybe it could help bring them freedom. I would make my own dress. I would also blog about it every day like Elaini did, complete with a charming photo of me in the dress. I would put up a Facebook page too. And then I would ask people to partner with me by giving money to organizations that were already working to help people coming out of human trafficking.

As Mom and I discussed different options, my plan began to take shape. It was going to happen. The dream of the dress was born—or maybe I should say, the nightmare of the dress. Well, the nightmare of the making of the dress. Here I am, three months later, sitting at the dinner table still trying to figure out how in the world I'm going to make it work. Who knew sewing a dress could make you feel so incompetent? Dad finishes his prayer and passes the platter of steaming chicken.

"What about dress number two?" Mom asks.

It's always been my plan to sew two identical dresses, just in case something happens to one of them. Now, though, I'm closing in on my February 1 start date and still haven't finished the first dress. Things aren't going quite the way I had planned. Sewing a custom-made dress is not as easy as I thought it would be. It may be time to lower my expectations a little.

"I think I'm going to be doing well if I can get the first dress done," I say, wiping my fingers on a napkin. "I've given up on being able to sew a second one."

That decision might come back to haunt me, but for now I need to back off a little on my grand plan. I can't even think about sewing a second dress at this point, seeing as the first one feels like it might end me. I take another bite of chicken. Maybe some protein will give me the focus I need to figure out the buttonholes.

When dinner is over, I head back to my room and my sewing project. I lift the fabric off the machine and run my fingers over the stitching. I let it drop onto my desk. Protein or no protein, I don't have the energy to sew anymore. I have no idea how I'm going to finish. I sit down on my cedar chest and reach across to my bed for Mom's old laptop. Maybe watching the recording of the message Christine Caine gave at the Passion 2012 gathering yesterday will inspire me to sew. She's an abolitionist and cofounder of the A21 Campaign, a nonprofit focused on ending human trafficking. I turn on the laptop. Little do I know that the next forty-five minutes will be exactly what I need to put the last touches on the dress.

2

Why Didn't You Come Sooner?

Passion 2012 Gathering

The cursor circles in an endless color wheel as I wait for the web-page to load. This week, thousands of college students are gathered in Atlanta to worship, learn, and give. Passion Conferences holds a gathering at the beginning of each year. This year the organization is live-streaming the sessions and leaving them up online for a day, so I'm catching as many as I can.

I click on Christine Caine's photo, and a video player pops up. While it's buffering, my mind starts to wander. It's strange how God works sometimes. I wasn't always passionate about ending human trafficking. I knew it existed, but in junior high and my early high school years, my focus leaned more toward children's ministry and dance.

Anytime I could, I would dance. I took a few classes each week, but I also loved to just dance around the living room. My favorite was pointe class. Nothing compared to the thrill of moving with precision and skill through a piece of music. I wasn't the most graceful dancer, but I loved the physical feeling of a job well done. I felt myself come alive as I moved. Around the time I started dancing, I noticed that something was wrong with my foot. I kept at it though. Before too long, the pain made dance challenging. Even walking hurt.

Two years ago, I finally found out what was wrong. That day was the beginning of the end of dance for me. I met with my doctor and, with the help of an X-ray, learned I had Freiburg infraction in my right foot. Basically, the top of my second metatarsal and the base of my second toe had jagged edges. There wasn't enough cartilage to cushion the bones when they rubbed together, and the doctor couldn't do much about it. The disease often affects young females, and there are different theories as to why this happens. The doctor left it up to me whether or not I wanted to keep dancing. He said it wouldn't make the infraction any worse. The decision simply came down to how much pain I could stand.

My head was spinning when I walked out of his office. I couldn't imagine life without dance, but I was tired of being in pain. I didn't know it yet, but the challenges with my foot were only the beginning of a growing number of health problems I'd face. Just six months after that appointment, I decided to stop dance classes. We tried surgery a little while later to smooth out the joint and move the cartilage around, but it didn't help. The pain was too much, and my classes were over my head. It was time to let dance go. However, giving up my dance classes eventually opened a new door for me. As that dream was dying, God was giving me a new passion.

The webpage loads, and the roar of the crowd at the conference brings me back to the present. Even though it's a recording, I can feel the energy coming through the screen. Christine Caine is on stage. She and her husband, Nick, started A21 with the goal of abolishing slavery in the twenty-first century. They work toward this goal by raising awareness, providing a safe place for rescued women, and using education to preventing trafficking.

I slide onto my bed and pull the laptop closer to me. The intensity of Christine's voice and the urgency of her tone draw me in.

27 million people woke up in slavery today.
Every 30 seconds, someone is trafficked.
Only a few of them are ever rescued.[1]

As Christine talks about trafficking, I feel my stomach twist. How could anyone do that to another human being? People made in the image of God should never be treated like property, never tricked or coerced into forced labor and prostitution. Her voice grows soft as she tells about a group of rescued women who were living in a shelter in Thessaloniki, Greece. Christine sat with them and shared her own story of abuse and how God had redeemed her. She told them that he could redeem them and make them new too.

As Christine shared with them, one of the women interrupted and asked, "If what you're telling me about your God is true, then why didn't you come sooner?"

Christine pauses, swallowing her rising emotions. The stadium is silent. I brush the tears out of my eyes.

Why didn't they come sooner? Why didn't someone rescue her earlier? How can we claim to know a God who loves all of his children and yet let such injustices keep happening? Why aren't we doing something? Anything? These questions race through my mind as Christine challenges the students to take action in response to the stories they've heard. She says we can all play a part in stopping modern-day slavery.

The dress is my "something." It's my voice raised in protest. I won't wait another minute. I click open another tab and type in the address to my blog. Creating a new post, I let all the emotion and urgency of Christine's message spill on to the page. I invite people to join me on this journey of working to put an end to slavery.

People who have been trafficked can't wait another day. They can't wait for us to wrap our minds around this dark reality that seems so far removed from our daily lives. Human trafficking is a growing problem throughout the world, and millions of people are desperate for freedom. We should be just as desperate to help them.

I publish my post and get back to work on the dress. They can't wait and neither will I. Twenty-four hours later, the dress is finished. It's not what I had imagined, but it's ready for me to wear. It's pretty loose—in some spots, it feels more like a sack than a dress. If anyone looks too closely, they'll see slipshod sewing and uneven seams. It's no work of fashion, but the last buttonhole has been sewn, the last tuck has been made, and the skirt has been hemmed. I wander around the house in a daze. The weight of the project is slowly sinking into my heart. The dress is really done. And I'm really going to wear it for a whole year. Jason Gray's "Jesus, We Are Grateful" streams through my headphones, and my heart echoes each thank-you he sings.

Still, I can't get Christine's words out of my head. February 1 is too far away and too long to wait. A new date comes to mind: January 11. Human Trafficking Awareness Day. It's less than a week away. The next morning, I talk with my parents and Tori and ask them if I'm crazy to want to move my start date. They tell me to go for it, so I announce it on my blog.

I may not be dancing anymore, but I'm on the move. All the passion God has given me will be spent on this project. My hopes and dreams for this year have been sewn into the stitches of this dress. Next week, I'll put it on and step into this journey. I can hardly believe what I'm about to do.

January 9, 2012
Two Days!

The Facts: In 2014, the International Labor Organization estimated that forced labor generates $150 billion in profits a year worldwide.[2]

One Dress. One Year. For Freedom.

Is it just me, or is this crazy? I feel like I fast-forwarded through three weeks. Honestly, when I first started thinking and talking about this idea, I didn't think I was actually going to do it. But here I am, two days away. And the cliff is looming ever closer. That's okay though because Mom told me the other day, "If you're going to fail, fail while daring greatly. Fall off a cliff, not a curb." So here's to the cliff and all the exciting adventures coming in the next year!

Also, IJM sent me an email the other day. Last year the organization rescued 1,600 men, women, and children from slavery and violent oppression.

One more thing: Wednesday is Human Trafficking Awareness Day. There are twenty-seven million slaves in the world today, and most people are unaware. So what can you do? Wear orange. Orange is the color of human trafficking awareness. Tell someone about human trafficking. Until they know, they can't act.

January 11, 2012
Day 1

Outfit: black dress, orange long-sleeve sweater with white trim, black flats

The Facts: A person doesn't have to be moved from one location to another to be trafficked.[3]

Total Raised: $65

One Dress. One Year. For Freedom.

Well, here it is . . . Day 1. I can't believe it. I feel like I've run out of words to explain what this experience means, but know this: I'm beyond excited for this year. I hope you are too. Will you take a minute and give to freedom? Your prayers and money make a huge difference.

Also, something else really cool is going on tonight as part of Human Trafficking Awareness Day. Zach Hunter and Compassion International are hosting a Twitter chat about human trafficking. If you have questions about human trafficking, come join in.

Are you wearing orange for Human Trafficking Awareness Day?

3

Going Public

Day 1
Valencia College—Not My Favorite Place in the World

Today is the day. January 11, 2012. Day 1. My stomach has been doing flips all morning. I rub my damp palms on the stiff, dark material of the dress as I get out of the van. I'm anxious about wearing the dress, but I'm more anxious about attending my classes at Valencia College. I tug on the bottom of my bright orange sweater that's trimmed in white, trying to smooth it out. I don't really like the way my body looks, and the thought that so many people are looking at full-body pictures of me on my blog today doesn't encourage me. I wish I could feel confident and comfortable about the way I look, but no matter how hard I try, I keep comparing myself to other girls I know—ones who I believe look better than I do.

This sweater was the only orange thing I could find to wear today. At the beginning of the project, I decided that I wouldn't purchase any new clothing during the year. Many people who are trafficked for labor are forced to work in sweatshops to make the clothes we find in stores in the United States, so I'm trying to keep my slavery footprint to a minimum. Made in a Free World, an organization whose goal is to empower individuals, groups, and businesses with innovative solutions to end slavery, has developed a survey to help people understand how their purchasing habits and the products they buy are connected to slavery.[1] The survey calculates a person's slavery footprint—the number of slaves who work to make the things they consume. Every time I take the survey, I feel sick to my stomach. I've decided to stick with what's in my closet or my friends' closets this year instead of buying anything new. I'm just grateful that my friends own a lot of cute clothes. Today's sweater belongs to my mentor, Pastor Sylvia, who's the children's pastor at my church.

I lock the van and walk toward my Spanish class. This is my second day of class this semester, and on a campus this large, I don't expect to find a friendly face. I step onto the curb and make my way through the school's wide-open corridors. The brick buildings jut up against a bright blue sky. It's warm for January, and the humidity is making my tight curls frizz. I push down the fear that wells up in my throat whenever I walk this campus. I'm only here two days each week. The rest of the time, I'm homeschooled. Earning college credit in high school is great, but most of the time, I wish I could do without these two days at Valencia. I'm a fish out of water. Today, I'm a bright orange fish out of water. I wonder if anyone knows that today is Human Trafficking Awareness Day or that people are wearing orange to commemorate it.

A slight breeze ruffles my skirt as I open the door to one of the student lounges. My Spanish class meets in an adjoining classroom, so the only way I can get to class is to walk through a crowd of college students. I step in, pushing up the sleeves of my sweater. I can't tell if I'm warm because I'm nervous or because I have on two layers. Either way, I'm warm.

I stand outside the door waiting for class to start. Through the small window in the door, I can see the class before mine wrapping up. A few kids gather at the computers behind me. Across from me, a couple whispers forehead-to-forehead, fingers intertwined. Two older women sit nearby chatting with one another. Valencia is open to people in the community, so the age range in our Spanish class is wide. One of the women, dressed in cozy sweats and a T-shirt, looks at me. *Is it possible that she knows I'm wearing orange for a reason? That would be amazing.* I smile at her. She smiles back.

"I love that color," she says, motioning to my sweater.

"Thanks. I'm wearing it because today is Human Trafficking Awareness Day." I'm hoping to start a conversation about it with her.

"Oh." She looks at me blankly. "I thought maybe you were wearing it to support that teacher in the news."

"No." I shake my head, hesitating. "I haven't heard about that."

"I guess people are wearing orange to support her. That's why I thought you were wearing it."

What a weird coincidence.

Just then, the door opens and students stream into the lounge. *Thank goodness.* I feel the warmth from my sweater creep up into my face. I didn't expect that response. She was completely indifferent. I don't know what I expected. Maybe a "That's great!" or "It's cool that you care about that."

I slide into a seat in the front row and pull my notebook out of my backpack, giving myself a silent pep talk. *Not everyone knows about modern-day slavery, and not everyone cares about it like you do. This is just the beginning.* Now to other important things: How is this class going to go? The syllabus makes the professor sound really uptight, and Monday's class didn't make him seem any more relaxed. I just hope everyone I run into today isn't as indifferent to my project as my friend in sweats. Otherwise, it could be a very long day.

Youth Group—One of My Favorite Places in the World

The sun dips low in the sky as Dad pulls up to the curb to drop me off at youth group. I can't believe my first day in the dress is almost over. I survived my morning classes at Valencia and spent most of the afternoon on the computer anxiously watching for blog views, Facebook likes, and new donations. I tweeted and posted on Facebook to remind everyone that today is the first day of The Dress Project. A momentous day. There weren't any new donations, though, so it wasn't momentous in that way.

Many encouraging messages have poured into my in-box, but I was hoping more people would donate money. I'm wearing the dress to help people see how important it is to end human trafficking. I want what I'm doing to inspire them to *do* something. Still, today's only Day 1. I hum Josh Wilson's song "I Refuse" under my breath as I walk across the cobbled patio outside the youth building. It's become my theme song. It's about refusing to do nothing about the injustices in our world. I'm not waiting around for other people to do something. I want to make a difference. Thinking about today and my awkward conversation at Valencia makes me wonder what kind of difference I'm going to make.

As I pull open the door, laughter and shouting spill out. This church is my second home. I know every inch of it. In the last five years, I've spent countless hours volunteering with the children's ministry. My best and worst moments have happened here. It's where I first came to know Jesus and where I've been coming to know him more ever since. I check my name off the attendance list in the entryway and step into the main room. It's small group night, so there aren't too many kids. The middle school boys yell, chasing one another across the black-and-white checkered tile floor. A few adult leaders group chairs together and joke with the kids. As I look around for my friends, I'm blindsided by a bear hug.

"Wow!" I laugh, squeezing my friend Erin, trying to keep both of us upright.

"I can't believe you're actually doing it! The dress! I love it!"

I push her back and twirl around, giving her the full 360-degree view of my ensemble.

"How's it going so far? Is it good? Is it weird? Have people said anything?"

Her excitement helps me get excited again.

"Yes, it is good. And yes, it is weird. It's both. Today I had a lady at Valencia ask me if I was wearing orange in honor of some teacher. That was awkward."

She laughs with me, and it lights up her beautiful freckled face. Her vibrant red curls bounce all over the place.

"Do you already have your outfit picked out for tomorrow?" she asks.

"Yep. Tori came over last weekend and helped me plan my first twenty outfits, and on Sunday my dad took pictures of me in each of them. That way I can schedule each day's outfit ahead of time to post on the blog first thing in the morning."

"Morgan!" Erin shouts. I turn toward the door. I hadn't seen Morgan come in. She whips her head around, and her long brown curls follow. She's a few feet away talking with Jarrod, our youth pastor. Erin and I walk over to them.

"Bethany! You're in the dress. I can hardly believe you're really doing this!"

We both giggle. The dress is a bit surreal for all of us. Morgan is another one of my best friends. She and Erin share my passions for children's ministry and dance. We became close because of all the hours we spent working at church and dancing together.

As I start telling Morgan about my day, Jarrod heads to the sound booth to make sure everything's ready for tonight. Samantha, his fiancée, sits poised on a bar stool at the table I'm leaning on. She's also a student at Valencia, and she has her laptop open to work on homework.

"Bethany," she says, "I know you're wearing the same dress for a year, but I don't exactly understand why. Aren't you doing it to raise money or something? How does it work?"

"Well, yeah. I'm wearing this dress all year. I'm trying to raise awareness about human trafficking and money to end it." I can tell I'm butchering my description, but I'm not sure how to be clearer.

"How will wearing the dress raise awareness though?"

"Well, I have a blog dedicated to the project. Each day I'll wear something different with the dress and post a picture of my outfit. I'm also using the blog to ask people to give to International Justice Mission."

"Okay," she responds slowly. "But why the same dress every day?"

If this year is going to be successful, I need to learn to explain the project better. "Well, it's tied to slavery in a small way. Enslaved people wake up and face the same reality day after day without any hope for escape. My dress is a tiny way for me to help do something about that. It's not the same thing at all, but I figured that I can certainly wake up to the same dress every day for a year if it will help them wake up in freedom one day."

Something about what I say clicks. "Oh," she says. "That's amazing!"

"Yeah, that is really cool, Bethany. I love that you're pursuing this passion that God's given you." Jarrod's voice startles me. I've been so busy explaining my project to Samantha that I didn't see him walk up.

"I should post a link to your blog on Facebook," Samantha adds. While we've been talking, she's been looking at my blog posts. "How's this?" She points to the text on her screen.

Click on the "How It Works" tab to find out why she's wearing the same dress every day!

"That's great," I say, smiling. "Thank you so much."

"You're welcome. Just keep me updated about how it's going, okay?"

"I will."

I can feel the anxiety of the day slip away. Suddenly I don't feel as worried about how people will react to the dress. The people who matter most to me are cheering me on. A sense of peace settles in. This is what I'm supposed to be doing. It's not going to be easy. I'll probably encounter a few more people who have weird reactions this year. But the dress is starting conversations and giving me an opportunity to share my heart and passion for freedom. It's also allowing me to invite others on this venture as we try to make a difference together.

A shrill bell interrupts my thoughts. "Okay, everyone! Gather up. We have a lot planned for tonight," Jarrod yells across the room. Erin, Morgan, and I grab our bags and head to the front.

I breathe a sigh of relief. I have survived the first day. I can do this. It's going to be fine—at least until I go camping next week. I'm not sure how camping and the dress will mix. The dress and camo? The dress and crawling around in a tent? Maybe it's best not to think that far into the future. I should just enjoy this moment. Settling in to my seat, I think about the day. I can't believe I'm doing this for real. *Okay, Jesus. Show me how you want me to live this out.* I've found myself praying something like this off and on throughout this week—and really, since last fall when the idea of the dress started to become reality.

It seems like a simple prayer. However, I can't help but feel that this journey will turn my life inside out . . . and it's only Day 1.

January 17, 2012
Day 7

Outfit: black dress, brown sweater tank, black flats

The Facts: 126 million children work in hazardous conditions, often enduring beatings, humiliation, and sexual violence at the hands of their employers.[2]

Total Raised: $165

One Dress. One Year. For Freedom.

You know what my favorite thing is about the outfit I'm wearing today? My good friend Tori made the sweater. She's the same friend who came over to help me put together several outfits, most of which you'll see in the first two weeks of the project. I doubt this would even be happening without her prayers, support, and encouragement.

Actually, this whole project is a patchwork of people who have supported, encouraged, prayed for, advised, and helped me in so many other ways, and I'm beyond grateful. It's amazing how God has chosen to use people in my life in such powerful ways. So to all of you—you know who you are—thank you so, so much.

4

Camping in the Dress

Day 8
Blog Headquarters

Mom turns on the kitchen faucet and plates clatter together as she slides them into the sink. I watch her from the computer desk in the living room, feeling a twinge of guilt. I should be helping, but tonight she's letting me off the hook so I can write my blog posts for the next few days. I'm going camping this weekend, so my posts need to be done before I leave. Camping in the dress will be interesting. Then again, I'm finding that most things I do in the dress are interesting.

Twice a year, a group from our church goes camping. Pastor Sylvia organizes the trip. Most of the families who go have kids or teenagers involved in my church's youth ministry. My parents will be on a work retreat this weekend, so Pastor Sylvia has invited me to be a temporary member of the Ragsdale family and join her, her husband, Andy, and their five-year-old daughter, Veronica, on the trip. We're going to Kelly Park, which is about an hour from my house. Rock Springs feeds into Rock Springs Run and winds through the park not far from our campsites. I can't wait to jump into the cool, clear water at the springhead and then float down the run with my friends. First, though, I need to finish these blog posts and pack. I sink against the back of my computer chair and put my feet up on the wall. Tilting the monitor toward me, I pull the keyboard closer and sigh. I wish blogging wasn't so difficult. I didn't know when I started the year just how hard it would be to come up with something new to say every day.

I scroll through my file of photos. The dress with a teal jacket, the dress with a red bandanna shirt, the dress with a gray long-sleeve shirt layered underneath. Dad took each photo of me in the front yard. He used to be a photographer, so he knows his way around a camera. I have to wonder what the neighbors think I'm doing, though, when I pose out front with different outfits on. The pictures blur together, and I try to rub the sleep out of my eyes. I probably shouldn't have waited until the last minute to pull these posts together.

The dishwasher beeps and whooshes as Mom starts it. "Good night, Bethany," she says and heads down the hall.

"Night, Mom."

The house is quiet. Michael's back at school, and Mom and Dad are getting ready for bed. As the silence settles in, I begin to wonder if these outfits are going to be practical for camping. *Am I going to be able to pull this off?*

As I scoot back to sit up, my chair creaks in protest. I pull my feet down off the wall. Wrenching my mind back to the task at hand, I upload each photo and add a few sentences. After hitting the "schedule" button on all four posts, I lean back and stretch my neck. Done and done.

Dad comes out to turn off the lights. "Oh, I didn't realize you were still up."

"I'm just finishing my blogs for this weekend."

"Okay," he says. "I hope you have fun camping."

"Thanks." I look up. "Have fun on your retreat."

"We will. Good night." He bends down and kisses my forehead. "I love you. Turn the lights out when you go to bed."

"Okay. Love you too."

I grab a pen and a piece of paper. Scrolling through the photos again, I make a list of the clothes I need to pack. It's a short list. Wearing the dress makes some things harder, but it sure makes packing easy. I grab the canvas duffle bag I left on the kitchen table and head back to my room to gather everything on my list. I toss in my swimsuit, pajamas, and toiletries, and set the bag by my bedroom door. Let the fun begin.

Day 9
Kelly Park

Kelly Park is absolutely beautiful. People come here year-round to camp under the towering oaks and huge sweetgum trees. They also come to swim in the sparkling springs. In January, the mornings are cool, but the air warms up as the sun peeks through the leaves on the tress. The campsites are arranged around a circular road. About thirty of us are camping together this weekend. Our neighboring sites line either side of the road.

When my family goes camping, we keep it simple. On the contrary, from the electric blankets and space heaters to the multiple grills and coolers set up under a screened canopy, camping with the Ragsdales is like living in luxury. There's no family I'd rather be with. We spend the first afternoon setting up. The Ragsdales' site is the center of the action, and as dusk fades to dark, families gather at their campfire to get warm and catch up by the dancing flames.

Shouts of laughter chase smoke into the sky. S'mores are the order of the evening. We crowd around the fire in folding chairs and hoodies, licking melted chocolate off our fingers. I duck in my seat as a blackened marshmallow hanging off a wire swings past my face. At the other end of the long fork is a middle school boy. "Be careful, son!" his dad calls across the fire.

"Sorry," he says, grinning at me. I smile. Campfires and middle school boys could be a dangerous combination. I load another marshmallow onto my roasting fork and stick it in the flames.

By the time the fire has died down to just a few embers, most people have trickled back to their campsites and gone to bed. I look across the fire at Pastor Sylvia.

"Well, I think I'm going to turn in," I say, standing up.

"Good night, Bethany. Good work. Sleep well." She smiles from under her hoodie. "I'll most likely kill you in the morning."

I laugh and shake my head at her reference from *The Princess Bride* as I wander over to my tent, unzip it, and crawl inside. I have the best pastor in the world. I slide into my sleeping bag as fast as possible, trying to stay warm. *I'm glad I brought jeans for tomorrow's outfit.* If it stays this cold, I may need to wear all of my outfits at once. I try to think warm thoughts as the murmur of crickets lulls me to sleep.

Day 10
Very Cold Two-Man Tent

On Friday morning, I wake up to the savory aroma of bacon sneaking through the seams of my tent. The tarp rustles as I roll over. I open my eyes a sliver and then shut them again. I wonder if bacon is a good enough reason to get up and venture into the chilly morning air. I burrow deeper into my warm cocoon of a sleeping bag and before I know it, I drift back to sleep.

Somebody shouts across the campsite, jolting me awake. As soon as I'm out from the sleeping bag, I start shivering. My breath forms cold puffs in front of my face. I reach for my duffle and dig around until I find my jeans. I slip into them, pull the dress over my red shirt, and belt it all together with a wide brown belt. A blast of frosty air takes my breath away as I unzip the door. I reach back, grab my jacket, and duck out of the tent. After zipping it shut, I head over to the fire.

Veronica is sitting at the table eating breakfast. She looks up at me, takes in my outfit, and asks, "Are you wearing that *again*?"

Five-year-olds tend to say whatever comes to their minds.

"Yes," I say to her. "I'm wearing it again. And again. And again. I'm going to wear it every day for a whole year." I slide in across from her at the table.

She looks at me, eyes wide. "Really?"

"Yes, really." Or at least, I hope. I hope I make it through the whole year. But I don't tell her that part. Each morning this week as I've put on the dress, I've wondered if I actually *will* make it. At the same time, I'm amazed that I'm doing this project in the first place. Bethany Winz, the girl who is great at starting things but not always great at finishing them, is committing to something for an entire year. I sewed the dress, I've kept up with my blog, and I'm wearing the dress every day like I said I would—even on a camping trip. I may not be Christine Caine, but I'm doing something. I may not be in the slums of India, but I'm still trying to change the world—or at least my world. I just hope I can help other people think seriously about human trafficking and inspire them to act.

A few hours later, our group is circled around the fire again when Andy asks, "Who wants to go swimming in the springs?" Kids scatter in every direction to get their swimsuits. I walk back to my tent and change into mine. The springs flow out of a giant cavern and into a stream that has carved a path through the center of the park. The water runs fast and clear, making it perfect for tubing. I can't wait to jump in. Kids swarm the picnic table as we wait for Andy. I have my swimsuit on with a pair of shorts over it. My towel is draped over my arm.

One of the moms looks at me. "Wait. Where's the dress?" she asks.

I smile. "It's in my tent."

"So you're not going to wear it when you go swimming?"

"Nope." I laugh. No one wants to see my dress float to the top of the springs. I may be dedicated, but I'm not that dedicated. Besides, I would hate for anything to happen to it.

Some of the middle school kids have joined us. "What about sleep? Do you wear it when you sleep?" one of them asks.

"Nope."

"Do you wear it when you shower?" another asks.

"Nope. I wear it only when I would wear normal clothes."

I guess I'm not the only one making a huge adjustment. I may be the one wearing the dress every day for a year, but all of my friends are trying to figure out what that means for me and for them.

I hear another car pull up. I turn, hoping that it's Morgan or Erin, but the car passes our campsites and disappears around the bend. I hope they get here soon. The day won't be complete if I can't enjoy the springs with them . . . and maybe tip them over.

The unblemished spring water pours over the rocks. The sound of it mingles with howls of joy and the plop of inner tubes hitting the water. The stream winds through the park, ending in a huge, roped-off pool of water. The head of the springs is our favorite spot.

"Come on, you guys!"

I scurry up onto the wide rock and push back the mass of wet hair dripping in my face. Erin and Morgan follow me out of the water. They're finally here. It's my second trip to the springs today. Now that they're with me, all is right with the world. We walk to the edge of the rock. The spring bubbles out of a cave to our right.

"Are you ready?" Morgan asks.

"Yep." I wrap the strap of my underwater camera case around my wrist, take a step back, and launch into the air. Angling myself between the rocks, I shoot down into the water.

As I come back up, Erin yells, "Move over. It's my turn!"

I swim to the side and dive down, camera poised. She plunges in and pauses at the bottom for her photo. Bubbles trail from her mouth and nose. Above the water, we let the current take us a few feet downstream so Morgan can jump in. I snap a photo of her too. Another group of kids disappears around the bend, floating happily on inner tubes. They'll ride down, grab their floats, and head back up to the top to do it all over again. A few kids use the wooden stairs that lead down the bank to get into their tubes, but most jump off the outcropping of flat rock that serves as a dock.

The water, carrying quite a few people, laughs and sings over the rocks on its way to the bottom of the park. Our group stays at the springhead, and my friends and I stay with them. My underwater camera has made me popular with the other kids. A splash overtakes me as another one of them jumps in, and I dive down to snap a photo. A chorus of "Can I see it?" greets me as I resurface. I laugh.

"Of course," I say, pushing a few buttons on my camera through the sturdy plastic sleeve. I hoist myself up onto a nearby rock, and the kids gather around, their faces eager to peek at the underwater pictures. It feels so nice to be out of the dress for a little while.

Our excitement reminds me of why I'm wearing the dress. Some people don't get a shot at this kind of joy. Every one of us should get to feel the warmth of the sun, the closeness of friends, and the freedom to do a cannonball in a Florida spring. Every one of us should have the chance to live with hope and be surrounded by love. In a few hours, I'll put the dress back on. But for now, I'm enjoying the freedom that comes with leaving it behind in my tent.

We grab some floats and head down the river with the rest of our group. The water propels us forward toward the end of the park. Today just keeps getting better. I've heard whispers of a huge game of hide-and-seek tonight. There's also a rumor of banana boats made with marshmallows and chocolate chips toasted in the campfire. My stomach growls at the thought. I can't wait. This is going to be a great camping trip—with or without the dress.

January 22, 2012
Day 12

Outfit: black dress, blue hoodie, blue and white tennis shoes

The Facts: Restore International works to fight trafficking in India through investigations and surveillance. They work with local law enforcement to conduct raids on brothels that enslave underage children. Then they arrest the perpetrators and traffickers and rescue the children and place them in safe houses.[1]

Total Raised: $165

One Dress. One Year. For Freedom.

I hope you are having an amazing weekend. I know I sure am! But even in the midst of having fun, don't forget those who are not free to enjoy their lives as they please. They should be, and you and I have the power to help make it so. A few minutes, a few dollars, and you could change someone's life. Forever.

5

Cutting Out the Middleman

Day 12
Home Sweet Home

Quiet Sunday evenings are a rare gift. I usually have youth group, but it's been canceled for tonight because of the camping trip. I yawn and flop down on the couch, sniffing my damp locks. "My hair still smells like campfire," I tell Mom. She's on the couch across from me, where she settled after she and Dad finished unloading the car from their retreat. I got home from Kelly Park earlier in the afternoon. All three of us are tired and happy.

"I just hope the dress doesn't still smell like smoke when it gets out of the washer."

"Well, if it does, it'll just remind you of all the fun you had this weekend."

"Yeah. Or it will remind everyone in class tomorrow that I smell."

We're silent for a moment.

"How was your retreat?" I ask.

"We had a great time." She smiles. "When you have a few minutes, I want to tell you about a conversation I had with someone about your project. It doesn't have to be tonight though."

I perk up a little. I like to hear what people think of the project.

"No, please, go ahead. You've piqued my curiosity now."

"Well, during the retreat I talked with a friend of mine about your blog."

"Oh?" Usually when Mom tells one of her friends about what I'm doing, they're impressed. They say something about how amazing it is that someone my age is doing something so huge. I mentally prepare for another pat on the back.

"She runs some blogs that reach lots of students." I nod. "She had some suggestions for your blog that might help you reach more people."

My curiosity is suddenly no longer piqued. I clench my jaw. I know I should be open to advice, especially from someone who has as much experience as this woman does, but I've never been a fan of hearing suggestions from other people. *I can do it myself!* That's been one of my life mottos. It may not be the best motto to live by, but it's been part of my personality for as long as I can remember.

Mom tells me that I've been using that phrase since I was three. She calls it being "fiercely independent" and smiles like it's a good thing. The truth is that it's caused more conflict between us than anything else. I suppose it's been a good thing sometimes, but more often than not, it's gotten me into trouble. One morning when I was seven, I put my hair up without brushing it first. I couldn't do my hair by myself back then. Who am I kidding? I'm sixteen, and I still struggle with my hair. When I came out of my room that morning, Mom saw how much of a mess it was and marched me right back in to fix it. She won that round. Most of the time, even when I don't want to admit it, she's right.

It's been almost a decade since that battle, but I'm still fiercely independent. It doesn't matter if it has to do with my hair as a seven-year-old or my website as a sixteen-year-old, I still don't want to hear what anyone else has to say. This is *my* project. I want to do it myself. Mom can read my thoughts by the look on my face.

"You're tired," she says. "Let's talk about this in the morning."

"No, no. I want to hear it tonight." I might as well get it over with. The real problem is that I can't hear a helpful suggestion without taking it as personal criticism. I hate being reminded that I don't know everything. And for some reason, my emotions have been running high lately.

"Just remember, she knows what she's talking about."

I swallow. "Okay."

"She had some suggestions about your phrasing and your website formatting. Her main suggestion, though, was to not use FirstGiving to collect donations since they take a small percentage of everything people donate. She thinks it would be better if people donated directly to the organization you're trying to support."

FirstGiving is the site I'm using to track donations. It's a click of a button for the giver, and it makes it easy for me to see the progress toward my goal. I get an email each time someone gives on behalf of the dress.

"Well, how *should* I do it?" I snap. The laid-back feeling from the weekend is gone. My shoulders tighten.

My mom then goes on to ask if I could give directly to International Justice Mission. She also shares her friend's other suggestions.

"I don't know." I sigh, burying my face in my hands. I tend to get easily overwhelmed. The problem isn't these suggestions. It's my perfectionism.

"You don't have to do anything with this. They're just suggestions."

"Okay. Fine. I'll think about them. Maybe. I probably should just go to bed."

"Okay. I love you," Mom says.

"Love you too."

I walk down the hall, tense and frustrated. When I get into my room, I flop face-first onto my bed. Burying my face in my pillow, I sigh. This is the first time anybody's offered suggestions. And I know that mom's friend knows what she's talking about. Still, when someone gives me advice, it makes me feel like they're telling me what to do—even when they're not. It doesn't help that I keep thinking that I should be doing more for this project than I am. It's only been two weeks, and I already feel like I'm letting myself down. Maybe I'm even letting God down.

These days, it seems like mood swings are the norm for me. I'm constantly tired and overly sensitive. It feels like my body is turning against me. Is this normal for teenage girls? All of these issues piled on top of each other make me feel out of control. They fuel my perfectionistic tendencies. It's a vicious cycle. Maybe there's more going on inside my body than my frustration about this project. It sure feels like it.

I flip over onto my back and hug my pillow. My eyes follow the circle of the ceiling fan whirring in the air, and I take a few deep breaths. I shouldn't feel threatened every time someone makes a suggestion. They're excited about what I'm doing. They're trying to help me do better, not hurt my feelings.

Maybe Mom's right. Her friend does have a lot more experience than I do. Maybe I have this whole thing wrong. The thought makes me feel sick. *Maybe I need to learn to accept help and advice from other people—especially when it's something they know so much about.*

I mentally sort through some of her suggestions. On my giving page, I compare my year in the dress to a marathon, and I invite people to partner with and support me throughout the year by giving to International Justice Mission. She suggested taking that language out. I'd been thinking of it more as a walkathon than a marathon, but I'd used the wrong wording. Maybe I will just remove it. She also suggested changing the phrase "men, women, and children" in slavery to just "women and children." I'm definitely going to leave that one as is since men are trafficked too. But her suggestion to give all the money to International Justice Mission makes sense to me. I want every cent I raise to go toward ending slavery.

It's going to take some time for me to process her suggestions before I make any adjustments though. Right now what I need most is sleep. I'll be able to think more clearly in the morning.

Day 13
Same Living Room, Different Attitude

On Monday morning, I bounce into the living room. "Mom, I've got it!" A good night's sleep has me thinking in new ways.

"Got what?"

"I think I've figured out how I want to handle fund-raising."

She looks up from her laptop. "Yeah?"

"I was thinking that I can have people give directly to an organization and then email me with the details about their donation. If I do that, then I can give them several organizations to choose from."

"Huh. That sounds like it could be really good."

I plop down in front of the family computer again. Curling my legs up under me, I turn on the screen. "Now I just need to figure out which organizations to direct people to."

I pull up my WordPress dashboard in one tab and my "How It Works" and "Give Now" pages in two others and start playing with the formatting. Before I know it, I've implemented several of the suggestions Mom's friend offered, and my blog is looking much better. A few months later I do decide to add a comparison to a walkathon when a family tells me they're donating a dollar a day for the year that I wear the dress.

I click over to my FirstGiving fund-raising page. A few months ago when I emailed IJM and asked if there was a way I could track donations for my project, they recommended FirstGiving.

However, now I'm not so sure that was the best idea. I scan the giving page on IJM's website. I'll probably miss a few donations by asking people to donate directly and then let me know, but at least none of the money will go to a middleman.

I start bringing up the websites of other organizations on the screen.

- the A21 Campaign
- Not for Sale
- Love146

Each of them has a slightly different mission, but all of them are working to end slavery. Some focus on rescuing and rehabilitating trafficking survivors. Others provide social entrepreneurship opportunities for communities. A few focus specifically on prosecuting traffickers and providing survivors with legal counsel. Most play a role in all three aspects.

The list doesn't feel complete though.

I add Compassion International because it concentrates its efforts on fighting poverty, which is one of the leading causes of slavery. Armed with a list of five incredible organizations, I go to work on my "Give Now" page and update it with links to each one.

As the week goes on, I remember one more organization I have run across in the past few months: Restore International. It has a leadership academy in Uganda. It also helps to house girls coming out of sex trafficking in Uganda and fights to free girls from slavery in India. A few days later, I add brief descriptions of each organization to the page so that people have the information they need when deciding which organization to give to.

My fund-raising goal—$100,000—is still the same. But now it involves a variety of organizations. It's about encouraging people to give to whichever part of the anti-trafficking movement moves them the most.

The things that move people's hearts are the things that are going to move them to donate. We spend our money on what we care about the most. In order to successfully end a problem as huge as human trafficking, all of us have to get involved. I hope this moves people's hearts. Let the giving begin.

January 23, 2012
Day 13

Outfit: black dress, purple bandanna top, denim jacket, black flats, silver hoop earrings

The Facts: The average age of a trafficking victim is twelve years old.[1]

Total Raised: $165

One Dress. One Year. For Freedom.

I hope you all had as wonderful of a weekend as I did! A group of families from our church goes camping periodically, and it's always a delightful time. During the trip we took this weekend, we played hide-and-seek, swung on swings, pushed kids on swings, saw lots of smiles, made s'mores, got eaten by bugs, played in the springs, went down the river, took underwater photos, and did all sorts of other fun things. There was much to enjoy.

Have a happy Monday!

6

A Heart-Breaking Party

Day 13
The Think Tank

Tori sits back in my desk chair. I flip open Mom's old laptop on the bed beside me. "Let me see if I can find this email," I say, staring at the screen. "I have another idea for us."

"Uh-oh," she says.

But I know she's on board with my plan before I even tell her what I'm thinking. She's always been my partner in crime. Most of the ambitious things I've done, from homemade cosmetics to an after-school ministry for kids we tried to start in middle school, have had something to do with Tori.

A few years ago Tori and I decided that because we and most of our friends were single, we should get together on Valentine's Day, eat chocolate, and watch *I Love Lucy*. "I loved that Valentine's Day party we pulled together," I tell her. "What if we threw another party this year, but this time it will be a party with a purpose?"

"I like where this is going," she says. "Are you talking about the Love146 party?" Love146 is one of the organizations I'm asking people to donate to this year. In February, they encourage supporters to get together for a celebration of broken hearts. "When is a broken heart worth celebrating?" they ask. "When it changes the world."

"Yeah. They emailed me about it in January. The whole idea is to have people come together to let their hearts be broken by human trafficking and then to celebrate those broken hearts by doing something to end slavery."

We spend the rest of the afternoon making party plans. I pull up the organization's website, and together we watch a video of Rob Morris, one of the founders, as he tells the story behind Love146. In 2002, while Morris and the organization's cofounders were in Southeast Asia on an exploratory trip to find ways to fight child sex trafficking, investigators took them undercover to a brothel where they witnessed children being sold for sex.

I fight back tears as he explains that they named the nonprofit after a girl they had seen in the brothel. She was one of many. Each girl had a number pinned to her red dress. They sat behind a pane of glass watching cartoons as men stood on the other side and took their pick. One girl in particular caught the attention of Rob and the other members: #146.

I see Tori swallow hard, fighting back her own emotions. So many of the girls they saw had lost the will to fight. Pain and despair scarred their youthful faces. But the girl labeled #146 was different. She still had fight left in her eyes. Morris explained that because of how the operation was set up, they weren't able to do anything that day. When the brothel was finally shut down, the girl with #146 pinned to her dress wasn't there anymore. But her story and the number she wore left a lasting impression on them—so much so that they made her number part of their name.[1]

My mind is racing with ideas. Tori and I agree that we want to be part of what Love146 is doing. We brainstorm about invitations and baked goods for our own Celebration of Broken Hearts. I text Erin and Morgan and ask if they'll help with the party.

My phone vibrates twice. Two texts saying, "Yes!" Tori has a busy schedule for the next few weeks, so it's going to take all four of us and our ideas and time to pull this off. It's time to throw a Valentine's Day party that will make a difference.

Day 39
Love146 Celebration of Broken Hearts

Saturday, February 18, dawns bright and clear. It's a perfect day for a party. I handed out invitations a couple weeks ago. Inside each envelope was a construction-paper heart that opened down the middle with a zigzag cut. The front read: "When is a broken heart worth celebrating?" The inside offered Love146's answer: "When it changes the world." Specific details regarding the party were tucked snugly inside the invite. I just hope the invitations made a strong enough impression to motivate people to attend. I glance at the clock. I need to get myself ready—my friends should be here soon.

Stepping out of the shower, I dry off and slip into the dress. As I button it up, I go over the program for the party in my head. *I'm going to show that video of Rob from Love146, Tori's going to talk about how the porn industry increases the demand for sex trafficking, and Mrs. Molly, Mom's friend, will share details about her visit to House of Hope, an aftercare facility for trafficking survivors.* I pull my damp hair into a low bun but wait to put on my pink and silver fringed scarf. I have a morning of baking ahead of me, and fringe and frosting don't mix well.

I walk out to the kitchen to get to work. The carrot cake balls that took Morgan and me two tries to get right yesterday are chilling in the fridge. The mini cupcakes sporting tiny flags with #146 on them are ready on the counter. All that's left is to bake the sugar cookies we mixed last night, rearrange the furniture in the living room, and set the table. The doorbell rings. Morgan's coming over early to help me finish baking and decorating the cookies.

"Coming," I yell, my bare feet slapping against the wood floor as I run to the door.

A few minutes later, we're neck-deep in pink sprinkles. The kitchen bears the mark of great bakers at work. I wipe down the counter with a Clorox wipe and then a wet paper towel. Instead of using flour to roll out the cookies, we're using powdered sugar. Opening the bag, I sprinkle it across the counter. Morgan drops a blob of dough in the center. We roll it out and use heart-shaped cookie cutters to make the cookies.

After sprinkling each cookie with pink or red sugar, we slide them onto a cookie sheet and put them in the oven. I set the oven timer and step back, surveying the mess we made. Cleaning up is the next order of business. My eyes meet Morgan's. The white powder covering the counter is sugar. A smile tugs at the corners of my mouth. "Do you want to lick it off?"

She raises an eyebrow. "Okay."

As we lick our way down the counter, our noses send puffs of sugar fleeing before us. Once we've licked up most of it, I wipe down the counter with another Clorox wipe to remove the rest of the sugar and any residual spit. As I turn to throw the wipe away, Morgan and I make eye contact again and burst into laughter. We splash water on our faces to remove the last traces of sugar.

She takes a deep breath. "I can't believe we just did that."

"Me either. Just don't tell my mom, okay?"

"Okay."

The oven timer blares. I pull the last batch of cookies out and line them up on a wire cooling rack. Morgan walks over to the table and centers the glass vase, which serves as our donation jar, on the smooth white tablecloth. We arrange the food around it. Pink mini cupcakes, carrot cake balls, and red and pink sugar cookies. Even the food has a Valentine's Day theme.

"Is there anything I can do to help?" Mom asks, coming into the kitchen. She has on a red top.

"Can you cut up the strawberries and put them in a bowl?" I ask.

"Yep." She pulls the strawberries out of the fridge and starts washing them.

The doorbell rings again. Tori, Erin, and Tabitha are here to help finish setting up. "What else needs to be done?" Tori asks.

"Can you and Erin push that couch up against the wall under the window to open up the room?"

I slide the coffee table closer to the couch, and Tabitha and Morgan arrange the rest of the chairs in the empty spaces in the kitchen and living room.

"It looks great," I say as I survey the room. "Thanks, you guys."

The open floor plan of our house is perfect. As soon as people come in, their attention will be drawn to the kitchen and the table of goodies. I'm not above buttering up people with delicious food. The work that Love146 is doing is worth it.

Around three o'clock, people start to trickle in. I grab my scarf from my room and loop it around my neck to complete my Valentine's Day look. My stomach feels a little weird. It's just nerves, but it probably isn't helping that Morgan and I licked a whole counter of powdered sugar. I've invited about thirty people, but only a dozen have told me they're coming. I'm hoping more will show up. My friend Allison and her mom walk in the door, and I hug them. A few more of Mom's friends follow them in. Mom is across the living room laughing with Mrs. Molly, who has recently returned from a trip to Nicaragua. While she was there, she visited a home for girls who are survivors of trafficking.

As I walk back into the kitchen to check on the food, I hear someone say, "These carrot cake balls are delicious!" Making the carrot cake balls with Morgan was a small catastrophe. Many of them had crumbled into a million tiny pieces by the time we were done. I doubt we'll ever make them again, so I'm glad people are enjoying them.

I balance a paper plate with a few strawberries on it in my hands and survey the room. It's a smaller crowd than I'd hoped for, but everyone seems excited. Erin and Tori are standing by the piano discussing what they're going to talk about. I walk over to them and set down my plate.

"I'm going to get started. Are you guys ready?"

"Yep."

"Okay. Let's do this." I turn to face the open room.

"Hey, everyone." The buzz dies down. "First of all, thank you so much for coming to our Celebration of Broken Hearts. We're about to get started, so grab a drink and feel free to have a seat."

Morgan dims the lights, and I pull the video of Love146's story up on Mom's laptop. The background music swells as the presentation begins. Even on the small laptop screen, the story of these women is powerful. Several ladies wipe their eyes as the image of a girl with #146 flashes by. I've seen this video several times, but I still feel a familiar lump in my throat. This is why we're throwing this party. This is why I'm wearing the dress.

After the video, Tabitha, Morgan, Erin, and I share statistics about trafficking and the work of Love146. Tori talks about the pornography industry and how it connects to sex trafficking. Then Mrs. Molly shares what it looks like in Nicaragua to help someone heal after their life has been shattered by slavery. The pictures she shares from House of Hope are a story in themselves. Real people who have found real hope—that's what this party is about.

As the last picture fades from the screen, I invite people back to the table.

"You probably know that one of the reasons we're throwing this party is to raise money for Love146. If you'd like to give, you can leave your donations in the vase on the table. We want to let our broken hearts change the world."

Several people drop donations in the jar and grab another treat before they head out the door.

"Thanks so much for coming," I say, handing each person a baggie as they leave. The bags are filled with broken pieces of candy hearts. They're a reminder for people to let their hearts break about human trafficking. Each one has a card with information about Love146. Mom hugs Mrs. Molly and thanks her one more time for coming.

As I shut the door behind the last guest, I let out my breath. It's just me and my friends. Morgan yawns, leaning on Allison. Her mom and my mom are in the corner catching up. It's been a long, full day. Tori starts pushing the furniture back into place. I dust a few cupcake crumbs off the table so I can dump out the donation jar. I sort through the assortment of bills, checks, and change.

"You guys," I say, my voice catching in my throat. Everyone looks at me. "Wow, $591. We got $591."

"Yay!" Erin cheers. Tabitha gives me a high five.

This is the most money I've collected at once.

"That's amazing!" Tori says, smiling.

I'm thankful I didn't have to throw this party on my own, and I'm thrilled that we raised almost $600. But another thought keeps nudging me. *What could I have done to get more people involved?* I feel my excitement waver a little as I grab the empty cookie plate and take it to the sink. I'm still so far from my goal. It seems impossible to raise $100,000 right now. *Why didn't more people show up? Don't they know what's going on in the world? Don't they want to stop trafficking? Should I have invited more people? Different people? Who?*

I reflect on the day and Love146. The money we raised is only a tiny drop in a huge bucket of need. *Will it even make a difference?* I wonder. I wipe some frosting off the front of my dress.

Does what I'm doing even matter? I keep my thoughts to myself. I don't want to be a downer after everyone has been so kind and done so much work.

"Bethany, can you help me?" Tabitha is using all of her weight to try to move the couch back to where it belongs. It won't budge.

"Yeah. Hold on!"

I grab the corner of the couch, and we lift it across the wooden floor. Setting it down, we collapse onto it together. For the first time today, I relax. *Is The Dress Project actually changing anything?* I wonder. *Is it changing me?*

February 24, 2012
Day 45

Outfit: black dress, blue flower skirt, yellow cardigan, black flats

The Facts: In 2012, the International Labor Organization estimated that there were more than four times as many children trafficked for labor than for sex.[2]

Total Raised: $1,377.50

One Year. One Dress. For Freedom.

I opened the cabinet door on Wednesday afternoon and was immediately faced with a decision. In Florida, cockroaches abound, so I wasn't entirely surprised when I found one staring back at me. However, I was tired, so I really just wanted to shut the door again and go back to what I was doing. The problem with that, though, is I knew that if I didn't face the roach at that moment, then I would probably face him later. Isn't that how things work? So I pulled over a chair, grabbed my shoe, and began pulling things out of the cabinet. Mom came into the kitchen and asked me what I was doing.

"I'm writing a blog post," I said.

Of course! Because I usually write my blog posts while standing on a chair in the kitchen looking into a cabinet. But in all seriousness, I started thinking about this little roach and the lessons he was teaching me. When I'm exposed to evil, I want to do the same thing. I want to close the cabinet door and pretend I never saw it in the first place. The problem is that I did see it. I know it's there. That makes me responsible. If I don't face it, then who will?

William Wilberforce, a British politician, philanthropist, theologian, and abolitionist, once said to the members of Parliament prior to voting on his abolition bill in 1789: "You may choose to look the other way, but you can never again say you did not know."[3] Slavery still exists, and you know about it. Will you face it? Will you do something?

7

Not for Sale

Day 57
Clase de Español

It's never good when you can smell yourself. Never. One of the perks of the dress is less laundry. The drawback, though, is that I have to do it more often. Unless I forget, which can lead to smelling myself. Of course, when you wear one thing every day for two months, it starts to smell a little funky no matter how well you wash it. That's where the dress and I are right now as I walk into Spanish class. I scoot into a plastic chair in the front row and pull out my notebook from my backpack. A hint of sweat and old deodorant catches me off guard as I uncap my pen. My professor is starting class. Several classmates walk in late and take their seats. I refuse to make eye contact with anyone, hoping that the other students will keep away from me. The appeal of doing something as over-the-top as wearing the same dress for a whole year is beginning to wane, and I'm only two months in. Ten long months of black-dress days stretch out in front of me. How do you say "my dress is smelly" in Spanish? *Mi vestido es maloliente. Did I conjugate that right?* I sigh. Today is going to be one of those days: a stinky-dress day. It's not the first, and it won't be the last.

I can hardly focus on what the professor is saying. This weekend is my birthday. It's also the Leadership Rocks conference. A bunch of youth leaders from my church's children's ministry are going down to the conference in West Palm Beach. I love birthdays and conferences more than conjugating verbs. I let my thoughts wander and begin writing a packing list on a blank piece of paper in the back of my notebook. The music this weekend is going to be incredible. The Museum, the band that's playing, has one song in particular that resonates with me. It's called "Not for Sale," and it's the song that links my heart and my smelly dress to their music. They wrote the song because they've been working with the nonprofit organization Not for Sale to raise awareness about human trafficking.

I hope I'm able to tell them about the dress. I already know what I'm going to wear to the concert. Last Christmas I received the band's T-shirt, which reads "This Shirt Frees Slaves." I'm going to wear it with a white skirt and layer the dress on top. I'll wear the dress open, though, so people can see my shirt. After I wash the dress, that is. You can't really celebrate your birthday or meet members of a band you like in a dress that reeks. I glance up at the clock and tap my pen on the edge of my paper. Let the countdown to the fun—and laundry—begin.

Day 59
Leadership Rocks Conference, West Palm Beach

Music pulses through the speakers in the crowded sanctuary. The church is massive. The lights are bright. Hundreds of voices fill the lobby as we exit the broad doors from the main sanctuary. A horde of teenagers hyped up on music and more than a little sugar swarms the tables of the different bands and ministries at the conference. Morgan, Erin, and Erin's little sister, Amanda, are with me as we weave our way through the crush of kids. I spot Pastor Sylvia and the rest of our group huddled in a corner. Grabbing hands, we make our way to them.

Once we're out of the fray, Erin turns to me. "Are you going to ask the guys from The Museum to sign your shirt?"

"I'm not sure." I hesitate. "I feel like it might be weird."

"You should do it."

I look over to where the band members are standing. There isn't anybody in line right now. I feel a hand on my shoulder and a push forward. Leave it to Pastor Sylvia to force me out of my comfort zone. "Go talk to them," she says.

I grab Morgan and Erin and head over.

Four tall, young men are standing next to a table. They look like legitimate rock stars with their scruffy facial hair and edgy clothes. I'd gone down to the front during worship with my friends and a bunch of other teenagers, hoping to see them up close. Actually, I'd wanted them to notice me and to see that I was wearing their T-shirt. It wasn't particularly holy of me, since I should have been concentrating on Jesus during worship, but I'm not particularly holy most days. The stage lights were so bright and the sanctuary was so dark that they probably couldn't see me anyway.

I force myself to walk up and introduce myself to the lead singer. I see the shirt I'm wearing in a different color on the table.

"Hi, my name is Bethany," I say, sticking out my hand.

"Bethany, thanks for coming out," he says as he shakes it. "I'm Ben."

Erin and Morgan are right behind me.

"I just wanted to tell you that I love your song 'Not for Sale.' It's kind of a thing with me right now. I'm really passionate about ending human trafficking. That's why I'm wearing this shirt." I point to the words printed across my torso. "Actually, that's why I'm wearing this dress too."

"Oh, okay," he says. I can tell that he's trying to sound excited, but really, he's confused. *I need to get better at explaining what I'm doing.* I can feel warmth creeping into my face. I grab the sides of the dress and hold them up.

"I'm wearing this black dress every day for a year as a way to raise awareness and money to help end human trafficking."

He nods. "I see. Since you're wearing it open like a vest, I couldn't tell what dress you were talking about."

"Yeah, and I'm not always the best at explaining it. I'm two months into this crazy project. Only ten to go," I joke. I wonder if my face is as red as it feels.

One of the other band members leans in. "You're wearing the same dress for a whole year? How does that work?"

Erin jumps in. "She wears different accessories with the dress each day. Then she blogs about the day's outfit."

"Today I'm wearing it open. Some days it's buttoned up like a normal dress. Each day I change it up. Since people who are in slavery wake up and face the same thing day after day, I decided that the least I could do would be to wake up and face the same dress every day if it will help them be free. I'm using my blog and social media to raise awareness. I'm also asking people to give to organizations that fight human trafficking."

"That's amazing," Ben says. The other guys nod in agreement.

"Thanks." I smile. I'm starting to relax a little bit. "I just have one question for you guys."

"What?" the drummer asks.

"Will you sign my shirt?" It feels a little weird to ask, but I love that these guys are doing their part to join the fight against trafficking.

"Of course."

I turn around and slide the dress down so they can get to the back of the T-shirt. Ben uncaps the Sharpie in his hand and signs my shoulder. The other three sign across my back. I slip the dress back up, and Erin takes a photo of me with the band.

"It's really cool what you're doing, Bethany," Ben says. "Keep it up." Other fans are lining up to get photos and autographs.

"Thank you so much," I say.

Morgan, Erin, and I start working our way back through the crowd. As we step out the door and into the humid evening air, Morgan turns to me. "That was amazing!"

"I know, right?" I dance around in a circle.

My friends don't even blink. They're used to this. I'm glad we're all cramming into the same hotel room tonight and that I get to wake up with them tomorrow for my seventeenth birthday.

This was the perfect way to start the weekend. It's a reminder to me that what I'm doing matters. And it doesn't just matter to me—other people are just as passionate about ending trafficking. While the dress is beginning to lose its novelty for me, it hasn't for other people. Seeing the looks on their faces when I tell them what I'm doing inspires me all over again. It's more than just a way to get attention. It's a reflection of how I feel about my life right now. Fighting slavery is worth every minute of wearing the dress. Even when I am sick of it—and its ten buttons and janky buttonholes. Even when it stinks, the dress and everything it stands for is worth it.

We meet up with Pastor Sylvia at her SUV. The darkened outlines of the palm trees that surround the mammoth parking lot press up against the night sky.

Glancing back over my shoulder and through the glass lobby doors, I see the huge banner announcing The Museum. Happy birthday to me.

March 17, 2012
Day 67

Outfit: black dress (worn open), jeans, white polo, green sweater, black flats

The Facts: The United States is a source and transit country, and it is also considered one of the top destination points for victims of child trafficking and exploitation.[1]

Total Raised: $1,843.50

One Year. One Dress. For Freedom.

Happy Saint Patrick's Day! Did you know that Saint Patrick was a child slave? When he was a teenager living in Great Britain, he was taken captive by pirates and sold into slavery in Ireland where he worked as a shepherd for six years. After he escaped, Patrick returned to Ireland as a missionary.

We are all called to different things in life. Fighting for the oppressed has become more and more trendy lately, but I hope that even if it wasn't, we would keep fighting. This isn't about what's fashionable. It's about justice. Enjoy your day filled with green, and take some time to learn a little bit more about the man for whom this day is named!

Did you see that we've reached $1,843.50 in donations? We're so close to $2,000! Will you help us get there?

8

Two Gifts, One Package

Day 69
How It Works

I love presents—especially when they come in the mail. Something about seeing a box with my name on it makes my heart race. When I walk in the door after getting home from Valencia, there it is—a brown box sitting on the kitchen table. "Bethany Winz" is stamped across the front. It's just waiting for me to tear into it.

"It came!" I shout.

I grab a pair of scissors from the kitchen. Mom walks over as I start to slice the tape.

"Careful," she says. "You don't want to break it."

"I know." I lift the flaps of the box. "I'm just so excited."

I know exactly what's inside—a new laptop. It's a family laptop to replace our old dinosaur of a PC, but my parents have agreed to let it be mine for the rest of high school. I ease the laptop from the packaging and set it on the table. Bubble wrap falls to the floor. It's beautiful. I can't wait to see what it does. I unwrap the cord and plug it into the wall. Within seconds, the welcome screen appears. I feel like a kid in a technological candy store. The keyboard is light to the touch and my fingers fly across it.

"It's so fast," I say, looking up at Mom. Of course, anything is fast compared to our family PC.

"I'm glad. I hope you love it."

"Oh, I think I do already."

A few minutes later, I pull up my email and blog. An unopened email from WordPress is at the top of my in-box. I click on it. Someone from Restore International left a comment on one of my blog pages.

Restore is one of the organizations I'm encouraging people to donate to. It was founded in 2003 by Bob Goff, a lawyer, speaker, and honorary consul for the Republic of Uganda. His first book, *Love Does*, is due out in a few months. It's about living a life of joy, adventure, and whimsy by loving one another. I can't wait to read it. He travels quite a bit, and it was during a trip to India that he witnessed human trafficking firsthand. Seeing such horrible and extreme human rights violations broke his heart. In response to that experience, he launched Restore International, a nonprofit that works to fight human trafficking by promoting human rights and education in India and Uganda.

I scan the email. My excitement builds as I click through to the page they commented on. The "How It Works" page explains The Dress Project and how people can donate.

> Every day, millions of men, women, and children wake up in slavery. Faced with the same bleak reality day after day, their dreams of freedom remain as just that—dreams.
>
> So for a year, I'm wearing the same dress every day. (Don't worry, though. I'll be sure to wash it. Sometimes.) I'll use accessories to create a different outfit each day and post a picture of it here on the blog. I'll be waking up to the same dress day after day, but it's something

I'm choosing. The reality that countless others wake up to day after day is the result of a choice someone else has made for them.

However, that's not the only reason I'm doing all of this. My experience and my feelings don't matter if they don't change anything. That's where you come in. Funding is key to the success of any organization, and we can make it happen. I'm wearing the dress, but I'm asking you to donate. It's kind of like a walkathon, but instead, I'm wearing a dress. You can sponsor me by giving to one of these organizations. You can do a dollar a day ($366), a dollar a week ($52), or anything else you'd like to.

You can provide hope and freedom for someone who is in slavery. It only takes a few minutes, a few dollars, and you could change someone's life. Forever.

Tucked under my explanation is a comment.

Thank you, Bethany, for what you are doing! We just received a donation in your name and posted about it on our Facebook page: http://facebook.com/restoreinternational. You are making a huge difference and are an inspiration! Best wishes this year as you make a stand for freedom. Thanks for the honor of including us! Restore International

I clap my hands together. This isn't new-computer joy. It's the kind that comes from remembering that I'm not in this fight alone.

"Mom, come read this."

I turn the laptop around as she walks up to the table. She reads the comment aloud.

"That's so cool! This must have come from the donation we made earlier this week."

When people give me cash donations, I give them to Mom. Using her credit card, she makes an online donation to whichever organization the donor has picked. She often leaves a comment about my project with a link to my blog. Earlier this week, we sent our first gift to Restore International.

"I can't believe they actually wrote me back. And they put a link to my blog on Facebook. Nobody else we've given to has responded at all. This is so cool."

I click on the link in the comment. Sure enough, they posted my blog on the Restore International Facebook page. Social media is the main way I'm telling people about the dress, so I love it when others help me spread the word. I can't stop grinning. A little bit of encouragement goes a long way.

I don't know it yet, but this is the beginning of one of the closest connections I'll have with an organization during The Dress Project. For the first time since I began this adventure, I feel like I'm not invisible to the organizations I'm raising money for. To them, what I'm doing matters. It makes sense. I'm not just a donor or an email address. I'm a partner, taking a stand for hope and freedom. There's part of me that craves acknowledgment for what I'm doing. I want to be noticed and for someone to remind me that what I'm doing matters. Restore has given me that and more.

March 25, 2012
Day 75

Outfit: black dress (buttoned at the top), dress with green and blue swirls, black leggings, white heels, green purse

The Facts: Of the 167 countries evaluated in the 2014 Global Slavery Index, the Netherlands had the most comprehensive governmental response to human trafficking.[1]

Total Raised: $1,895.50

One Year. One Dress. For Freedom.

This seems a little crazy, but I've been wearing the same dress for seventy-five days. That's more than 20 percent of the year! But we're only at about 2 percent of the fund-raising goal. We still have quite a ways to go. I've had a lot of people tell me they have been inspired by The Dress Project. And I'm truly grateful for the words of encouragement. But my goal isn't just for inspiration or to have an experience. My goal is change.

This goal is not something I can accomplish on my own. In fact, it's far from it. Human trafficking will stop only if people like you get involved. You can pray. You can give. You can make a difference. Will you?

9

Just Call

Day 90
The Porch Swing

The front porch swing is my favorite place to relax. Our street is quiet, but watching the cars go by and listening to the rustle of squirrels in the trees make me feel connected to the rest of my neighborhood. It's way better than being cooped up inside. Most of what I do for The Dress Project—checking email, updating Facebook, editing photos, writing blog posts—is online. I don't always feel like I'm connecting with real, live people. Today I'm blogging outside on my new laptop to switch things up.

I turn off my music and slip off my headphones and listen to the gentle creak of the swing as I glide back and forth. I click the button on my blog to upload a picture of the outfit I'll wear tomorrow. Sometimes sending my heart into the blogosphere feels like emptying my dreams into a black hole. I've been wearing the dress for three months, and the novelty has given way to a steady resolve. No matter what, I'm going to get this done.

Meanwhile, our short Florida winter has given way to the humidity of spring. My unruly hair responds daily to the increasing moisture. More buns and ponytails are in my future. Pushing my hair up off my forehead, I pull up Twitter and tweet a link to today's blog. Tweets are hit or miss. Sometimes people respond. Sometimes they don't.

I check my email, looking for new donations. None today. Even though the excitement is wearing off, and the donations aren't coming in like I had hoped, I'm still amazed by how long I've stuck with my plan. Like dance, which I remained committed to until it was time to quit taking classes, social justice is a passion for me. But it's a little different. It requires different things from me. I danced for my own enjoyment. It fulfilled me and made me feel alive. While I'm enjoying parts of this project, I'm not doing it for my own satisfaction—or at least, I don't want to be doing it for my satisfaction, although sometimes my motives get mixed up. Each step of this journey breaks my heart a little more, a little deeper. It's easy to let myself get a little harder, a little more desensitized, and a little more distant with every story I hear. The pain is too much for me to comprehend.

But it's also this heartbreak that keeps me going. It's not about me. Maybe that's part of the reason I've been able to follow through. I feel like so much is riding on this experiment. I keep uploading pictures and sending blog posts into the black hole of the internet because it matters. It also keeps me on the lookout for people to connect with. When I find someone who is as passionate as I am about ending slavery, I feel inspired all over again.

When I followed Bob Goff on Twitter, he sent me his email address. It was an automated message for new followers, but it seemed like he meant it. I already feel connected to his organization, Restore International, after their comment on my blog a few weeks ago. Bob is incredibly busy with Restore and his day job as a lawyer, but he's down-to-earth and makes himself available to the people around him—even the ones he doesn't know. He doesn't let the enormity of human trafficking paralyze him. He just asks, "Well, what are we going to do about it?"

It's the end of my junior year of high school, so I'm starting to look at colleges. I want to spend the rest of my life working to end trafficking, but I don't know what I should study. I've been emailing a few people to ask for their input. I remembered Bob's invitation, so I emailed him. My mom exchanged a few messages with Bob on Facebook a little while ago, so I wasn't completely surprised when he emailed me back. Opening up the email thread, I read back through our exchange.

From: Bethany Winz
Sent: Monday, April 09, 2012 12:34 PM
To: Bob Goff
Subject: Thank you

Bob,

Thank you so, so much. I know you don't know me, but you have made a huge impact on my life over the last few months, both in words you've said and written (book excerpts and tweets) and in what you're doing with justice and Restore. And the communication you've had with my mom has also been encouraging.

I'm seventeen, a junior in high school, and looking toward the future. Human trafficking is an issue I'm really passionate about. Right now, that means wearing the same dress for a year to raise awareness about it. But God has also given me this crazy dream to open a home (or homes) in the United States for girls coming out of sex trafficking. So I'm curious, as someone who is involved in the work of justice, what would be your best advice for me? Also, I'm investigating college options. Do you have any suggestions for what I should look at or any idea of what I might need for my degree?

Like I said, you've been a huge encouragement. And I really can't wait to read *Love Does!*

Thanks again,

Bethany Winz
One Dress. One Year. For Freedom.

From: Bob Goff
Sent: Monday, April 09, 2012 1:38 PM
To: Bethany Winz
Subject: RE: Thank you

Hi Bethany,

I think what you're doing is just terrific! Well done.

What if you give me a call sometime and we'll talk? I look forward to it.

No dream is crazy. We opened a home last week in Uganda for young trafficked girls. Almost surprisingly, the key is just . . . start. Day 1: rent a house. Day 2: furnish it. Day 3: start finding the girls to fill it. There are a few more details than that, but not many. You have your family in your corner, so just start! Honest!

Bob

From: Bethany Winz
Sent: Monday, April 09, 2012 2:57 PM
To: Bob Goff
Subject: RE: Thank you

That would be wonderful. What days/times are best for you?

Thank you for telling me that my dream is not crazy and for the fantastic advice. I saw the video about the new girls' home. That's so cool!

My parents have been extremely supportive with where God has led me. I'm definitely grateful to have them in my corner!

Bethany

From: Bob Goff
Sent: Monday, April 09, 2012 6:38 PM
To: Bethany Winz
Subject: RE: Thank you

Keep getting great input from your folks, Bethany. They sound like they are nuts about you and very supportive. Let me know anything I can do to help. I don't make appointments with friends, so just call anytime during a weekday, and if I'm not in a meeting, I'd be happy to answer questions you might have.

You are going to do magnificent things with your life! It will be fun for all of us to watch!

Bob

At this point, I think the smile on my face is permanent. After getting up off the swing, I walk back inside the house and set my laptop on the kitchen table.

"What are you smiling about?" Mom asks, looking up from the stove. She lifts a pot lid, and the smell of chili wafts across the kitchen. My stomach rumbles.

"I still can't believe Bob wrote me back and told me to call him."

"When are you going to call?"

I slide into a seat.

"I don't know. He said to call him anytime, so maybe tomorrow or Wednesday. I want to think about what I'm going to say."

She gives the chili a stir.

"Just call him. It's going to be great."

I feel warm. Not because of the Florida humidity, but because my nerves are on overload. Why am I so anxious? Why do I feel like I might die a little when I call him? Bob might be the most encouraging person I've ever exchanged emails with. This should be fun.

"Okay, fine. I'll do it."

"Good."

"Okay," I say, not moving from the table.

"Just go." Mom grabs the phone from the kitchen counter and hands it to me. I dial his number, shut my laptop, and walk back outside. Sitting on the swing, I hit the talk button.

One ring. Two rings.

"Hello? This is Bob."

"Hi. Hello, Bob . . . um . . . this is Bethany. I'm Bethany Winz. I've been emailing you, and you told me to call, and . . ."

His laughter interrupts me.

"Bethany! Yes! I've been expecting your call. I love what you're doing!"

I'm pretty sure Bob Goff uses only exclamation points when he talks. I feel myself relax a little bit.

"Can I ask you a few questions?"

"Of course! How can I help you?"

He may not realize it, but he already has helped me. His excitement about the dress reminds me of why I'm doing this in the first place. Sometimes, all it takes is one person saying the right thing to reignite a flickering passion. I feel encouraged again about putting on the dress for another day as Bob and I talk. Nine more months of The Dress Project feels manageable when I remember how many people are committed to ending modern-day slavery. By the time we hang up, I'm excited not only about the rest of the year but also about what will come after the dress. I'm excited about the future. There's a lot of smiling happening today.

I'll need this encouragement as the project rolls on. There have been a few bumps in the road so far, but things are about to get even more challenging. I'll need to know I have people rooting for me—my family, my friends, even people I've never met before. They're the ones who will hold me up when things get hard.

April 15, 2012
Day 96

Outfit: black dress, green-blue shawl, brown belt, yellow flats

The Facts: There are two million children worldwide in the commercial sex trade.[1]

Total Raised: $1,895.50

One Year. One Dress. For Freedom.

This week, families in India were freed from slavery in a rice mill.[2] And now they're rebuilding their lives in freedom—all because of people like you. Thank you!

10

Ice Cream and Insults

Day 100
My Bathroom

Ten days after my call with Bob, life tumbles from that mountaintop into a valley. Every teenage girl has to deal with hormones. It's part of growing up. And most have issues with the way they look. Almost every girl wishes she could change something about herself. For many of us, there's more than one thing we want to change. Bad hair days, the dreaded unicorn zit in the middle of the forehead, and not being able to find the right outfit are things that plague girls my age. But the things I wish I could change go deeper than frizzy hair and out-of-style clothes. I feel like my entire body is working against me.

A few months ago, my doctor did some blood work to check if a hormonal imbalance is to blame for whatever has been giving me so much trouble. The tests didn't show anything, but I find myself wondering if they were accurate. The unruly emotions are just part of the problem. Over the last few months, I've started noticing excess hair on my face. *My face*. How is this even possible?

It's the morning of Day 100 of the dress, and I'm not sure how much I feel like celebrating. Quiet tears race down my cheeks as I stare at myself in the mirror. Turning on the faucet, I do the only thing I know to.

I run the razor up the delicate skin on my face and then study it in the mirror. *That looks like the last of it. Or at least, that's as good as it's going to get right now.* I squirt a dollop of lotion into my hand and spread it across my cheeks. Taking a deep breath, I brush the tears away. This isn't how it's supposed to be. I'm a seventeen-year-old girl, and I feel like I have more facial hair than most boys my age. I don't know what's wrong with my body, but I'm desperate to figure it out.

There are many things about this year and the dress that make me feel like I'm on my own. But this weird hair-on-my-face thing makes me feel isolated. Alone. My parents know about it. Morgan, Erin, and Tori have been sympathetic. But none of them know what it feels like, and none of us know why it's happening. It makes me feel like a freak. I make eye contact with my reflection. *Just focus on the good about today. One hundred days of wearing the dress is a pretty big deal. Celebrate it.*

I walk down the hall to the kitchen to get breakfast. As I pass through the living room, Mom looks up from the couch.

"Happy Day 100!" she says. "I loved the video on your blog this morning."

"Thanks," I say.

I put the first one hundred days of photos together in a video with Josh Wilson's song "I Refuse" playing in the background. I want people to be able to see the entire journey so far. I can't believe I've been wearing this dress for one hundred days. Even with my hormones in a jumble, I can't help but smile. The dress has motivated me to do more than I ever thought I could. I'd pictured this day in my head, but now, here I am. Day 100. Mom interrupts my thoughts.

"I know your dad is out of town, but do you want to go celebrate tonight?"

"Yeah, that would be fun. We should go get some ice cream."

"Sounds like a plan."

I'm always up for a celebration, especially when I have something this good to celebrate. It's going to be a great day. I walk through the living room and into the kitchen and pour myself a bowl of cereal before I start on the day's homework. Homework first, ice cream later.

Day 101

The World Wide Web

The sun filters through my blinds, casting striped shadows on my bed. I love homeschooling. Who else gets to sleep until 8:30 a.m. on a weekday? Doing schoolwork in my pajamas is another bonus. Yawning, I drag myself out of bed and wander out to the living room. After settling on the couch, I open my laptop to check my email and Facebook before I get started on homework. I probably spend too much time on social media. I blame it on The Dress Project, but really, I just like to see what people are posting. A picture on Facebook catches my eye, so I scroll back up to get a better look. The photo is of me and Mom at the ice-cream shop last night. My forehead crinkles, and I stare at the screen.

A girl I don't know posted the photo. It's only in my newsfeed because several of my friends commented on it. *Why did she post a picture of me?* I read the caption underneath. It's a cruel comment about how I look. Her words are like a knife to my stomach. I lean back, speechless, and feel my face get hot.

"Uh, Mom?" I pick up my computer and walk over to her desk. "Look at this."

She looks up from her computer screen.

"Wait. That's us." Her eyebrows raise as she studies the photo. She looks as confused as I feel. "But who posted it?"

My heart is pounding in my chest. I swallow the lump in my throat. "It was the girl who was working at the ice-cream store last night. It only showed up in my newsfeed because some of my friends commented on it and told her to remove the picture."

Mom looks at my screen again, reading the caption and all the comments. "I'm so sorry," she says, looking up at me. "I'm going to make a call." She reaches across her desk for the phone. A million emotions race around inside me. I'm angry and embarrassed. More than that, though, I just feel sad. *How could she be so cruel? Do I really look so different that a stranger would post a picture of me on Facebook?*

Dropping back onto the couch, I try to wrap my head around what's happening. I pull up my email and send Tori a note about it. I switch to my other open tab. It's a brand new song by Tenth Avenue North that the band posted this morning. I've heard a preview of it, so I already know it's about forgiveness. The timing almost makes me laugh despite everything I'm feeling. I hit play and try to let the song work its way into my heart. I can hear Mom in her bedroom talking on the phone. Her voice is tense, just like every one of my muscles. I close my laptop and set it on the coffee table. *Well, I don't think I'm getting much homework done today.*

"I'm getting in the shower." I say it out loud, to no one, really, as I walk down the hall. I just need to clear my head. I flip on the light and turn on the faucet to test the water temperature. I don't want to think about what that girl said. It has to be because of my face—the extra hair that shouldn't be there. My body is playing a sick joke on me, and I just want it to end. A sob catches in my throat. I want to feel normal again. Stepping into the steamy shower, the tears on my face mix with spray from the shower and wash down the drain. Sometimes I wish I could redo a day. Or a year. The triumph of Day 100 feels lost. Not even a hot shower can wash away the feelings that are rising up in my chest.

"I'm meeting with the manager of the ice-cream store and the girl who posted the photo this afternoon at four o'clock," Mom tells me later that morning. "You're welcome to come if you want, but you don't have to."

Her concern is written in the frown lines around her mouth.

"Okay. I'm not sure." I'm sitting on a step stool in the kitchen. I reach for the counter above my head and grab a giant container of bubbles. It's been sitting there since I won it at a church event. I unscrew the cap, pull the wand out, and start to blow.

Bubbles float across the kitchen and bounce off the cabinets.

"How are you doing with all this?" Mom asks.

"I don't even know," I tell her.

I blow into the wand again, and we watch bubbles hit the tile floor and burst.

"I called Dad this morning and told him what's going on. He's sad he's not here with you."

I do my best to smile.

"I also emailed Jarrod, Mrs. Michelle, and Pastor Sylvia. They're praying for you. And Jarrod said that when he saw the picture, he cried too."

Hearing that makes me want to cry all over again. I figured Jarrod had seen it, since Samantha was one of the people who'd commented. I'm grateful that I have so many people who care about me, but this is just hard.

The afternoon passes in a fog. Tori stops by with M&M cookies and a note full of love and encouragement. Mom and I meet with the girl and the manager of the ice-cream store. I can barely stand to look at her. I know that I need to forgive her, but right now my heart is too raw. She apologizes, and they give us a gift card to the ice-cream store to try to make things up to me. Her manager decides to give her a second chance and lets her keep her job. I'm glad, sort of. I would feel bad if she lost her job because of me. But I wish I could get a second chance too—a second chance at Day 100. Really, I'd just like a second chance at living in this body.

Sometimes it takes me time to process an event before I can really talk about it. It takes time to sort through the lies I've begun to believe about myself. More than anything, though, I just want to get past this whole ordeal. I don't want to have to think about what happened or the upheaval of emotions it has created. I don't want to talk about it with anyone. I just want to forget about it.

I know I'm surrounded by people who love me. I know it more deeply than I can say. But there's a whisper of fear in my heart. It's a question I don't have the courage to ask myself. *Am I really lovable?* When I look in the mirror, I wonder if the way my body looks makes me enough of a freak to prevent people from loving me. I think it's something we all fear—that something we've done, the way we look, or the family we were born into makes us unlovable. No matter what people say or how well they treat us, somehow this fear embeds itself into our hearts, draining us of hope and joy.

In that way, I wonder if many of us have more in common with those who are in slavery than we realize. Even in good circumstances, it's easy to feel worthless. We're all longing for a love to set us free. We're desperate for it. The fear that we're unlovable is a lie we spend our entire lives fighting in one way or another. We have to face that lie with the truth of who God says we are: loved. Wearing the dress seems to make the fight even harder for me. I don't really know why—maybe because it's put me in a somewhat public position—but what happened on Day 100 at the ice-cream shop is only round one of this battle.

April 23, 2012
Day 104

Outfit: black dress, coral cardigan, sea green scarf, silver sandals

The Facts: Since beginning work in Uganda in 2006, Restore International has helped more than 180 students receive an education, more than 300 children enter primary and secondary school, more than 25 students attend university, and more than 25 girls enter safe houses.[1]

Total Raised: $2,325.00

One Dress. One Year. For Freedom.

Yesterday in church the pastor talked about doubt and asking God for wisdom. The bulletin listed several quotes about doubt, including my favorite one from C. S. Lewis:

> We are not necessarily doubting that God will do the best for us: we are wondering how painful the best will turn out to be.[2]

Sometimes what's best is extremely painful, especially as we walk through it. But I'm grateful that he works *all things* together for good. Yes, it's difficult to understand sometimes. It's something I'm wrestling with right now. But whatever you're walking through today, remember this: God is doing what's best for you, even when it's hard to see.

11

A Weekend in Pennsylvania

Day 114
Somewhere over the Eastern Seaboard

For as long as I can remember, part of every summer has included visiting churches and hearing my parents speak about their ministry. People and churches in different pockets of the nation support our family and the work my parents do with Cru, formerly known in the United States as Campus Crusade for Christ International. Whenever we'd visit my grandparents in Nebraska or Pennsylvania, we'd stop at several churches that partner with our family so my parents could share with the congregations the details of Cru's ministry around the world and the people who were coming to know Jesus because of it. Michael and I would tag along. That's just part of what it means to be a Cru staff kid.

My parents are missionaries. They spent some time living in the Philippines, but right now Dad serves as editor of *Worldwide Challenge*, Cru's official magazine. In addition to homeschooling me, Mom also teaches writing classes to homeschool kids. Her goal is to develop training to teach Cru staff members around the world how to write. It's the work God has called them to, and they've set an example for our family through their willing obedience. They rely on the financial support of others to help them do their work. They live out their faith on a daily basis. The Dress Project makes me feel like I'm walking in their footsteps.

I reach up and adjust the air vent above my seat. The flight attendant is pushing the beverage cart past my row.

Leaning down, she asks, "Can I get you something to drink?"

"Sprite, please."

She hands me a plastic cup brimming with ice and soda. Turning to the row on the other side of the aisle, she asks Mom the same thing. I place my cup in the circular indentation in my tray table and turn back to my book. I'm in the middle of *Love Does* by Bob Goff.

This weekend I'm flying to Pennsylvania to speak about my project to a group of teenage girls at a conference for Action-Impact, Inc., a nonprofit Christian youth organization dedicated to helping kids have a personal relationship with God through Jesus Christ. I'm a little nervous. It doesn't bother me to speak in front of people, but explaining the dress is getting a little complicated. When I started this journey, I had a clear picture of how I thought this year would go. Unfortunately, it hasn't gone like I thought it would. A lot of people seem to be indifferent to what I'm doing. They're impressed, and I do enjoy hearing that. Still, I'm doing this because I want people to help me spread the word and donate, but they don't seem to think that human trafficking affects them. Part of me thought that if I did what I felt God was calling me to, then things would turn out the way I wanted them to. Even though I never said it aloud, I had secretly hoped that it was as simple as that.

This expectation hasn't been met on several occasions this year. Here I am, trying to do what God has laid on my heart, and I'm wrestling with my health issues, feeling isolated, and not raising as much money as I would like. It's frustrating, but I'm starting to come to some realizations. For example, I put so much energy into trying to make everything in my life perfect. If I pour all my passion into a project, then I want to see great results. It's hard to be passionate about what God has called me to when the results I'm getting don't feel perfect or even good. I don't seem to be making much of a difference. Some days I wonder if the project is even worth continuing.

These are the thoughts racing through my head at 35,000 feet as Mom and I wing our way from Orlando to Philadelphia. I glance over at Mom, who's reading a book. My tray table jiggles as we hit a pocket of turbulence. *I wonder how she's really doing.* A few days before we got on the plane, we got a phone call that my uncle Rex, Dad's brother, is in the hospital. He's had a lot of health issues building over the past few years, but this is serious. Dad took a detour to Nebraska on his way to a conference in Denver in order to be with him. I know Mom is worried. So am I. We decided to move forward with our travel plans anyway. It's going to be a full weekend. I'm speaking to the girls on Saturday morning, and on Sunday we're visiting a church that partners with my parents in their work with Cru. Mom and I are both doing the things God has called us to do, and both of us are feeling a little distracted. Like mother, like daughter.

Mom and I each have a row to ourselves, so she's too far away for me to ask her how she's doing, but I hear her let out a long sigh. I smile at her, and she smiles back. The window outlines a dark sky. The blinking red light on the wing is all I see. We probably won't get to the hotel before midnight.

I start thinking about this weekend and all the people I'm going to meet. I'm an introvert, so meeting new people can be exhausting. Usually, I'd rather talk to people than talk with them. A knot forms in my stomach. Why does it feel like a bunch of hard things always happen all at once? My ears pop as the fasten seat belt sign lights up again. We must be getting close to landing. I fold up my tray table and lean toward the window, watching Philadelphia appear through the clouds.

Day 116
Action-Impact Girls' Conference

The parking lot on Saturday morning is nearly empty when we pull in. I adjust my orange and yellow confetti scarf as I step out of the rental car. Today's yellow flats are my favorite shoes. I have added leggings to my ensemble so I'll be ready for the self-defense class that's part of the conference. I sling my backpack over my shoulder. Mom and I stayed in an airport hotel on Thursday night and drove to the city of Elverson on Friday afternoon. Now we're only a few minutes away from her hometown of Malvern. We spent last night with her good friend Amy. Amy is the one who invited me to come speak at the conference. It's amazing how relationships can thread their way through the years, holding people close in spirit even when they're far apart.

Even though they haven't seen each other in a long time, Mom and Amy pick up right where they left off. It reminds me of my friends back home. I wish they were here. I'm much braver with one of them by my side. I wipe my damp palms on my dress and take a deep breath in an attempt to prepare myself to walk into a room full of strangers. Trying to fit in and feel comfortable in a place I have not been before is never easy. Amy calls us over to her car.

"Can you help me grab a few of these centerpieces?" she asks.

I grab one of the flower-filled baskets from her trunk. We follow her through the double doors at the front of the building, up the stairs, and into a large hall. The murmurs of a few instructors echo off the walls as they set up for the first event of the morning.

I stop at the sign-in table by the door to fill out a name tag sticker and check out the different activities being offered. Each instructor will be leading a breakout session at one of the tables and teaching the girls different skills they can use. We each get to pick a session. I trail my finger over the lists and stop. I sign up for the makeup tutorial at table 3. After the breakout sessions, all of us will take a self-defense class. It's a good combo—choosing the proper foundation and mastering roundhouse kicks—that should cover all I need to know to make it through high school. I make my way over to table 3 and find a Mary Kay consultant waiting to lead the session. Amy sets a centerpiece in the middle of each table, and Mom walks toward me.

"Are you ready?" she asks.

I take a deep breath. "I think so. I'm a little nervous."

"You'll do great. And Dad said that Uncle Rex has been holding steady. I think things are going to be okay."

The room has been filling up. Instructors are ready and girls are taking their seats at the tables. I sit down and tuck the back of the dress underneath me, pulling my legs to the side. Mom walks back to her spot. Only a couple other girls are at my table, and none of them are sitting next to me. I fiddle with my phone, trying to look busy.

It's funny how I'm able to fold away so many different emotions, put a smile on my face, and pretend everything is okay. My sweaty hands tell a different story. I look at the table in front of me. Each place has a small mirror, a makeup palate, and some samples laid out. Taking a deep breath, I check my smile in the tiny mirror. *It's going to be okay, Bethany.*

The morning passes in a whirlwind of lip gloss, self-defense moves, and a fancy lunch of tea sandwiches and cookies. Before I know it, Amy's in the front of the room introducing me.

"Bethany's mom is a friend of mine," she tells the crowd. "I'm so excited for her to come share what God has been doing in her life these past few months. She's been on a unique journey of educating others about human trafficking and raising money to put an end to it. Bethany, will you come share with us?"

The girls clap as I make my way through the tables to the front of the room. A big screen flickers to life. My laptop is open on the table in front of me, and the video of my first 116 days in the dress is ready to go. My heart is racing, but I clear my throat and smile anyway.

"Hi, guys," I say. "As you know, I'm Bethany. Thank you for letting me come and share my story with you today."

A few of the girls shuffle in their seats. *I need to hit my stride here. I need to get into what I'm trying to say or I'm going to lose their attention.*

"Mrs. Hofbauer asked me to tell you about the project I'm doing. I guess it's not every day that you meet someone who's wearing the same dress every day for a year. And yes, I do wash it." They laugh, and I start to feel more at ease. Maybe it's going to be okay after all.

"I want to start by showing you a video of my year so far. It's a slideshow of all the ways I've worn the dress and how much money I've raised." I click play and music streams through the speakers as my video plays.

It's the video I made for Day 100, but I also added photos for days 101–116. As the music plays, each outfit I've worn pops up on the screen. In the bottom corner, the donation total counts up. Even with the pictures in front of me, it's hard for me to grasp that I've really made it this far. The video ends, and the girls offer more applause. I take a deep breath. *Here we go.*

"You may be wondering how I came up with such a crazy idea. Really, it wasn't my idea at all. When I was in middle school, I learned from a magazine article that slavery still exists. As time went on, I became more and more passionate about doing something to end it. I just never really knew what to do." As I tell the story of the dress, my own words remind me that even when I can't feel him or see him, God is somewhere close by. I end by sharing one of the most important lessons I've learned this year.

"I don't want you to leave thinking that to do what God's called you to do you have to wear a dress for a year," I say. "That's not it at all. I do want to ask you this though: What are you passionate about? What makes your heart beat faster? Often, those things are passions that God has given us. So what can you do about *them*? It won't look like what I'm doing. That's good. We're supposed to be different. But all of us were made to do something. And if we all do our part, who knows what can happen? Thanks for listening to my story and for having me here today."

The girls applaud. I walk back to my table as Amy comes up to close the conference. I slide into a chair next to Mom.

"Well done," she whispers.

I take a deep breath and, for the first time all day, I relax. I feel my heart slowing down as Amy asks us to bow our heads in prayer. My anxiety about meeting new people has given way to an opportunity to share my passion. Mom and I are learning a lot about prayer and trusting God, and it looks like my uncle is going to be okay after all. This weekend hasn't gone exactly how we thought it would, but that doesn't make it bad. Maybe life isn't so much about getting exactly what you want as it is about understanding that no matter what, when you're following Jesus, you're not in it alone.

April 23, 2012
Day 104

Outfit: black dress, green cardigan, flower scarf, black flats

The Facts: Child trafficking victims can be found laboring as beggars and restaurant or hotel workers, as well as working in the porn industry, factories or agricultural settings, or even nail salons.[1]

Total Raised: $2,325.00

One Dress. One Year. For Freedom.

Learning about injustice is naturally upsetting. But did you know that justice may be hardwired into our brains?[2] Pretty incredible, huh? I'm constantly amazed by how complexly we were created.

12

Hide-and-Seek

Day 121
The Wells' Living Room

For most of my life, I've been a jeans and T-shirt kind of girl. It makes getting dressed easy. I've never thought about clothes as much as I do now. I have to plan far enough ahead so that I have something to wear each day. Layers and accessories have become my greatest allies in making the dress look different every day. Other people's closets have become my stores. I've asked my friends if I could borrow their clothes while they were still wearing them. No one is safe. The craziest part of all is that I've enjoyed it. Today's outfit is a favorite of mine. My red bandana-patterned top is layered over the dress and under a denim jacket. Simple and cute. Of course, I'm not thinking about fashion as I crouch behind the couch. I'm thinking about where the other kids are hiding and how I'm going to hide decently while wearing a dress. There are definitely some things I miss about jeans and T-shirts.

We met the Wells family through church, and our families became fast friends. They have four kids, three of whom are still in elementary school. They will be moving out of state in a couple days, so Mom and I stopped by tonight to drop off dinner for them since they're so busy packing. "Maybe if we don't bring them dinner, then they won't be able to move," I told her. She laughed. No such luck. When we brought the food, they invited us to stay and eat with them. Dinner led to an impromptu game of hide-and-seek with all four kids—Nolan, a kindergartener; Lorelei, who's in second grade; Summerlyn, who's a couple years older; and Landon, a middle schooler. I was bested as soon as Lorelei came up with the idea.

"Nose goes!" she shouted. All four kids immediately touched their noses. Apparently that's how they determine who counts first. I was the only one not touching my nose.

Nolan pointed at me and giggled. "You're it!"

So here I am, crouching behind the couch, waiting for them to hide. I close my eyes and start to count. "One, two, three . . ." Feet smack against the wood floors as the kids scatter. "Fifty-eight, fifty-nine, sixty. Ready or not, here I come!"

I peer over the back of the couch. The room is empty. I creep down the hall and open the door to Summerlyn and Lorelei's room. A muffled giggle comes from the closet. I tiptoe across the room and peek around the door. "Gotcha!" I shout as Lorelei squeals. Before we've left the room, the other three have snuck out from their hiding spots and gathered in the living room for another round. As Lorelei starts counting, the rest of us slip away. At the end of the hall on the right, the boys' room stands wide open. I look in. A bunk bed—perfect for hiding under. I drop to the ground and slide underneath. *I'm not going to let this dress stop me from having fun.*

I hear a yell of, "Found you!" and "You're it!" followed by a groan and the patter of feet running back to the living room. I squeeze out from under the bunk bed and walk back into the living room for round three. I wasn't found, so my bunk-bed spot still seems like a safe bet. This time, as I slide under, I feel a tug. *Riiiiiiippp*. My heart jumps into my throat. The back of my dress is caught on the bed slats.

Please be my shirt. Please be my shirt. I pray the thin shirt I'm wearing over the dress is what ripped. *Maybe it's that*, I think. *Maybe it's not my dress, which I still have to wear for more than two hundred days.*

"Forty-five, forty-six, forty-seven." A voice drifts down the hall.

Trying my best to stay quiet, I slowly reach behind me to feel where the rip is. I find it. It's the dress. I lay my forehead on the floor and sigh.

"Ready or not, here I come!" Summerlyn yells. The boards of the hallway floor creak as she walks toward the back of the house. I see her feet as she steps onto the carpet in her brothers' room. I hold my breath. She bends over and, suddenly, her face is in front of mine.

"You're it," she informs me as she reaches down to tag me. I scoot out from under the bed and stand up.

"Okay." I laugh. "Look at this," I say, turning around to show her the rip. It's on the top layer of the back of my dress. At least the lining is still in place.

"Oh no!" Summerlyn cries.

We walk toward the living room. "All right, you guys. I'm it. You can come out now," I say. Landon, Nolan, and Lorelei emerge from various rooms.

"Okay, count!" Lorelei says to me.

"Just a minute. I have to go show my mom something."

Mom and Mrs. Wells are talking in the kitchen. "Hey, Mom, look at this." I turn so she can see the back of the dress.

"Uh-oh."

"Yep. That's what I get for hiding under the bunk bed. You know the worst part about it, though?"

"What?" Mrs. Wells asks.

"I didn't even win the round of hide-and-seek." They both laugh. "Anyhow, I'm it now, so I need to go count. After we leave here, can we go to the craft store to get material to fix it?"

"Of course," Mom says. The kids are calling me to count, so I rejoin them in the living room.

A few rounds later, Mom tells me it's time to go.

"Aw, man." Nolan comes out of the bathroom. "I had a good place too!"

"Where were you hiding?" I ask.

"I'm not gonna tell," he says, hands on his hips. "Do you have to leave?"

"I'm afraid so," Mom replies. "We need to go fix Bethany's dress, and you guys have packing to do."

Lorelei sighs. I'm sure the younger kids will be heading to bed shortly after we leave. I, however, have a long night of dress-fixing ahead of me. I would trade places with them in a second.

"Thanks for coming and for bringing dinner," Mrs. Wells says. The whole family follows us to the front door.

"Our pleasure." Mom hugs Mrs. Wells.

"We sure are going to miss you guys," I tell them, frowning.

Their silhouettes are framed in the doorway as we walk out to the car and wave good-bye. There's still a hint of light in the sky. Summer is just around the corner. Sliding into the front seat of the car, I turn and wave one more time. I'll miss those kids. I'm just glad we got in one more game of hide-and-seek.

Later that evening, armed with a sack of mending fabric from the craft store and some instructions from the lady at the sewing counter, I'm ready to work a miracle. But first, I need to get comfy. I pull off the dress and look at the rip for the first time. I'm thankful that I only ripped the first layer. I put on a pair of yoga pants and a T-shirt, grab my sewing kit, and head from my bedroom to the kitchen. I hope I'm able to fix the dress. *Please, God, let me fix it.* I have visions of wearing a shredded, safety-pinned dress for the rest of the year. It's not pretty. The ironing board makes a loud screech as I pull it open. The lady at the craft store demonstrated how to place the fabric on the tear and iron it. Spreading out my dress against the thin frame of the ironing board, I trim the ragged edges. I slide a piece of the mending fabric in between the torn parts of the dress and try to move it around. The torn layer won't lie flat no matter how much I smooth it. Exasperated, I plop down on the kitchen floor.

Just then, Michael walks in. He's home from college for the summer.

"What are you doing?" he asks.

"Having an emotional breakdown."

He looks at me, then looks at the dress in a crumpled, black heap on the ironing board, and then back at me.

"I'm trying to fix my dress. I ripped it playing hide-and-seek tonight."

He tries to hide it, but I can tell he's laughing. I start to laugh too.

"Only you," he says, shaking his head.

"Thanks a lot."

I drag myself up and give it another shot. This time, I grab my sewing scissors from the table and cut a gap in the lining. I attach the mending fabric from the inside. It works.

"Yes!" I do a happy dance.

After grabbing a needle and thread, I whipstitch the lining back together. Is it wrong to want to hug the dress? Seeing it back in the game and looking presentable gives me the confidence to continue for the rest of the year. My growing interest in fashion means that I want the dress to look good. Thanks to a hide-and-seek incident, I'm now a problem solver and a tailor. The dress keeps bringing out new qualities in me that I never knew I had. I just hope the sewing projects are done for the year. I throw open the washing machine and toss in the dress so that it'll be ready tomorrow for another day of wear . . . and another and another and another. One hundred and twenty-one days and counting.

May 23, 2012
Day 134

Outfit: black dress, green shirt, denim jacket, pink flower hair clip, black flats

The Facts: India has the largest estimated number of people in slavery, between 10.7–12.7 million.[1]

Total Raised: $3,480.00

One Dress. One Year. For Freedom.

Have I told you lately that I'm thankful for you? We're at $3,480, and I'm in utter disbelief. We're just twenty dollars away from $3,500. Twenty dollars that could help bring someone freedom. Remember that there are six organizations I've recommended giving to. All of them are doing incredible work and putting your donations to good use.

It's been an exciting first 134 days, but we're not done yet. This isn't going to happen without you. Right now we're at 3.5 percent of our fund-raising goal. Will you jump in? You know that slavery still exists, but what are you going to do about it?

13

A Teenage Stage Prop

Day 162
Kids-a-Flame Camp

I want to transform the world with the dress. I want to change how people view slavery, how they spend their money, and how they think about freedom. I want to help them understand the cruelty of sweatshops and forced labor, as well as the reality of where the items they buy come from and how they are made. I want to change how they think about abolition. It's not only an American Civil War–era movement. It's also a right-now movement. It's a battle people are still fighting—in the United States and all over the globe.

When I think about how much I want to do, I get overwhelmed. I don't know if my project is changing anyone else, but I know it's changing me. The past few months have peeled back the layers of my heart and given me a glimpse of who I really am—passionate, scared, perfectionistic, persistent, conflicted, and headstrong. The dress is inviting me to change. It's inviting me to let Jesus transform me into the person he created me to be. It's also opening new opportunities for me to share my experience. I'm doing things I never imagined myself doing.

For example, I never imagined being rolled out onto a stage in a giant plastic bin. That's what I'll be doing in approximately thirty-seven minutes. Right now I'm surrounded by hundreds of kids at summer camp. We're packed into the front of a church sanctuary. The worship band is playing their hearts out. Kids and adults alike have their arms up in the air as they sing. A few kids are jumping up and down. The energy is palpable. I push my hair behind my ear and sing the words on the huge screen overhead. This is an important night. Kids-a-Flame Camp has been a big deal for our church for as long as I can remember. This year is my eighth. I went as a camper for the first few years, but now I attend as a junior chaperone. Tonight Pastor Sylvia has asked me to be part of her sermon about Mary and Martha.

During his sermon last night, Pastor Dean, the children's pastor from a neighboring city, Tarpon Springs, brought out a suitcase full of props. Each of his points was illustrated by something he pulled out of the suitcase. Pastor Sylvia and Pastor Dean have a friendly rivalry, so she wants to top all of his props with a giant live one—me.

The music slows as the band moves into the next song. The kids around me start rocking side to side. This song is my cue. I slip down the aisle and across the back of the sanctuary. I look up at the balcony lined with the flags of different nations. I can see Mom and Dad sitting in the front row. Dad has his camera out to capture the evening. Back in the sound booth, Michael is helping run the PowerPoint presentation. I want to make them proud. Also, I want to not pass out from nerves or a lack of oxygen inside the bin.

I head back up the side aisle and through the door at stage right. Backstage, I can feel my pulse getting faster. Despite the quiet worship song, my nerves are taking over. I let out my breath.

I know I'll be fine, but the wait is killing me. I pace, folding and unfolding my notes. Straightening the piece of paper, I glance over my meticulous handwriting to make sure I have all the information I need and it's all readable.

"Relax," Eric says, surfacing from the costume room. Bonnie is walking behind him, pulling the bin. Bonnie works in the children's ministry at the church in Tarpon Springs, and Eric is a college student from my church. The two of them are helping manage the stage, and they're in on our big surprise. They were the ones who figured out how to make the bin roll. The only other people who know how I'm going to be introduced are my parents. I wanted Dad to be ready to photograph my entrance. I tried out the bin yesterday. It's a tight squeeze, but fortunately, I'm not claustrophobic. I can't wait to see how people react when I pop out.

I laugh. Relax? That's easy for him to say. I always say that I don't mind getting up in front of people, but maybe I do. Or at least this time I do. If there's any group in the world that I want to impress, it's this one. That's not just because my friends are in the audience, either. I feel like I've grown up under the leadership of those who run this camp. I have so much respect for them. If I screw this up, it's going to stay with me for quite a while.

"Let's go," Bonnie says. We head for the wings. We can see Pastor Sylvia from where we stand. She's sitting on the stage next to a pair of green foam Hulk feet.

"When we spend time sitting at the feet of Jesus," Pastor Sylvia says, "we can do what he's called us to."

Bonnie hands me a microphone, and I wrap my notes around it. "Are you ready?"

"I think so."

Eric lifts the lid off the bin. He holds it still as I climb in. Tucking the dress between my knees, I scrunch down into a fetal position. I hear the lid snap into place. A drop of sweat runs down my face and off the tip of my nose. I'm not sure if it's because I'm nervous or because I'm trapped in a plastic box at a camp on a summer day in Florida, but either way, I hope I can get out soon.

I jump a little as Eric starts rolling the bin. "Now, I don't have a whole suitcase full of props like Pastor Dean did." Pastor Sylvia's voice seems to be coming from somewhere far away. "But I do have this bin with one really cool prop."

She lifts the lid, and the stage lights burst into my dark world. I blink a couple of times and sit up. Turning to the audience, I wave. There's a roar of laughter as Pastor Sylvia helps me out of the bin. The kids in the front row are smiling from ear to ear. They probably wish they could come take a ride in my bin.

"Many of you already know her, but this is my friend Bethany."

Eric sneaks out with two wicker chairs and sets them behind us. Pastor Sylvia and I settle in for our chat. I smooth out the skirt of the dress as she begins asking me questions. Dad's camera lens winks at me from the balcony.

"Bethany's doing a really cool project that I want her to tell you about." Pastor Sylvia turns to me. "What is it that you're doing this year?"

Launching into the story of the dress, I feel outside myself. I begin to relax as I fall into a rhythm. How I decided to wear the dress, how I'm trying to raise awareness about human trafficking, how I take care of the dress—it all flows as easily as if Pastor Sylvia and I were sitting down to talk over coffee. She breaks in with a question.

"How have you balanced work and worship as you've done this?"

"That's a hard question." I pause. "I don't know that I've done that very well, honestly. But in a lot of ways, this project has forced me to rely on God more. I'm still figuring out what it looks like to follow him in this, but he's walked me through some pretty hard moments with the dress."

"One of those hard moments was on Day 100. Would you talk a little bit about that?"

I knew this question was coming, but I still feel a knot of anger form in my stomach. Day 100 is something I still don't like to think about. It's going to take a long time for me to fully heal, and until then, it's hard to know how to talk about it. But it's part of the story of the year, and it's part of who I am now. I take a deep breath.

"Yeah . . . that was a really difficult day. I had someone post a photo of me on Facebook. The caption was a really unkind comment about my appearance. I was completely blindsided. It made me wonder why someone would be that hurtful—especially someone who didn't even know me."

"You said you were blindsided by it. I find that often, when something tries to knock my focus from what God wants me to do, it comes from a place I'm not expecting."

"Yeah, I definitely think that's true."

"So how have you worked through it? Did it make you want to stop wearing the dress?"

"I don't think it ever made me want to stop. But it was hard to forgive that person. It still hurts to think about it. Every time I do, I have to forgive her all over again."

Pastor Sylvia directs the conversation back to human trafficking.

"How do you feel like these days in the dress have connected you to those who are in slavery?"

"Well, people who are in slavery don't have very many day-to-day choices. While what I've encountered doesn't come anywhere close to their experiences, I figured that limiting my clothing choices for a year would be worth it if it could help someone else be free. I know that Jesus wants to set them free, and he wants us to be a part of it. Whether it's talking about it or wearing a dress to raise awareness or giving money to organizations that help people escape slavery, no act is too small. I also know each of us has different God-given passions and gifts. We can all do something. God can do big things through young people."

"I believe that," Pastor Sylvia says. "Thanks, Bethany, for sharing your story with us today. Can we all give Bethany a hand?"

She gives me a hug, and I hug her back. I wave to the kids as I leave the stage and then wait in the wings as she closes the service.

The question about Day 100 still rings in my head. *Why does it still hurt so much?* I bow my head as Pastor Sylvia prays for the kids. I still have questions about what is going on in my body. I'm grateful, though, that God is with me in this journey. He's teaching me to look for his presence even during hard experiences, and he's altering how I see myself. He's using the dress to address the deepest issues of my heart. And in the journey ahead, he'll continue to expose them—the deep hurts, the big dreams, and the unspoken expectations. And he will keep walking with me, even when I can't feel him by my side.

June 20, 2012
Day 162

Outfit: black dress with bandana top underneath, black leggings, brown belt, brown flip-flops

The Facts: Only 1–2 percent of human trafficking victims are rescued.[1]

Total Raised: $4,156.00

One Dress. One Year. For Freedom.

Ending slavery means addressing the root issue, and that's exactly what Not for Sale is doing. Yesterday I talked about how many forced laborers there are in the Amazon, but that's not the end of the story. Recently, Not for Sale provided artisan training for 130 women in the Amazon, which will allow them more economic opportunities.[2] Your gifts can help make this freedom possible.

14

Halfway There

Day 169
Yet Another Doctor's Office

I'm still thinking about Kids-a-Flame Camp while I wait for the doctor. Pastor Sylvia's question about Day 100 is spinning in my mind. Day 100 has led me here. We're still searching for some answers as to why my body is freaking out, so I'm sitting on yet another strip of crinkly white paper waiting for yet another doctor. Mom's reading a book in a plastic chair tucked into a corner of the office. A month ago, I was diagnosed with mild psoriasis, an autoimmune skin condition. It's just one more way that my body is rebelling against me. The doctor who diagnosed the psoriasis has sent me to a specialist to try to figure out what's going on with my hormones. We're hoping that we'll be able to put more pieces of my health puzzle in place.

The door opens, and a young woman in a crisp, white coat walks in.

"Bethany, it's so nice to meet you." She holds out her hand. I shake it, and then she turns to shake Mom's hand. She flips through my chart and asks what's brought me in today, so I tell her about all my symptoms.

"Well, based on your symptoms, it sounds like you have polycystic ovary syndrome or PCOS. It's a hormonal imbalance that impacts a lot of women. We'll do some blood work just to be sure, but it would explain everything you've been experiencing."

"What does that mean?" I ask.

"It means your hormones are out of whack. This explains symptoms like the male-pattern hair growth. PCOS causes many symptoms in all different kinds of combinations. It can cause acne. It can also cause weight gain. It can even affect your moods and make you feel extremely lethargic."

With each symptom she lists, I feel like a puzzle piece is falling into place. Mom nods from her seat. I'm not going crazy. It's my body that's going crazy. I feel like I've been battling against an unknown enemy, but now that enemy has a name: PCOS.

"Let's talk about treatment and some steps you can take going forward," she tells us.

Mom continues asking the doctor questions as I let relief flood over me. These health issues have been a walk in the dark, but I see a light ahead. It's a tiny light, but it's still a light. Maybe now that I have a diagnosis, I can get on with enjoying life—and celebrating the dress. The halfway mark of The Dress Project is two weeks away. I can't believe it. I plan to commemorate the special occasion with dress-shaped cookies outlined in black icing compliments of Bethany and Morgan. I let out another deep breath. I think there's more powdered sugar and counter licking in our future. Enough with the doctor visits. It's time to have some fun.

Day 183
Poolside at Allison's House

Three consecutive cannonballs produce a tsunami-like splash in the pool. Shouts of laughter fill the air and lights glimmer off the water. A group of guys huddles around the snack table, eating chips and drinking soda. My youth group is hanging out at my friend Allison's house tonight, regrouping after a long day of kids' camp at church. Summer, for me, is a long string of camps linked together by pool parties and beach days. Sitting back in a deck chair, I laugh as Erin plunges into the pool.

What a great way to celebrate the halfway mark of The Dress Project. I'm not swimming tonight though. Changing in and out of the dress feels like too much of a chore. But it's nice to sit by the pool and relax. The dress cookies were a hit at camp. Now I'm spending the evening with some of my favorite people. Two middle school boys are standing close by and looking at me. I can tell they have something on their minds by the way they're grinning.

"I have a question," one of them says, leaning on a deck chair.

"Yes?" I say, my eyebrow raised slightly.

"Do you really wear the dress every day?" Both of them heard my talk at Kids-a-Flame Camp a few weeks ago.

"I really do."

"But do you wash it?" the other one asks.

"No. I've been wearing it for 183 days straight, and I haven't washed it once." They almost look convinced.

"Is that why you didn't go swimming tonight?"

"Well, it's part of the reason."

"If you'd gone swimming, would you have worn the dress?"

"No." I laugh. "I would have changed out of it and then changed back into it."

"So you don't actually wear it all the time?"

"Were you at Kids-a-Flame?" Albert cuts in. I didn't notice him standing behind us. Albert, a twentysomething elementary school teacher, has been in town helping our church with camp this summer. He grew up in one of the churches associated with Kids-a-Flame, so we've known him for quite a while. Both boys nod. "And were your ears working?" He leans a little closer.

"Yes," they say in unison.

"Then how could you not know when she does and doesn't wear the dress?"

I laugh.

"Okay, so what if the dress gets stained?" one of the boys asks.

"Well, I wash it."

"What if it rips?"

"That happened already. I just fixed it."

The what-if questions get more and more outrageous until Albert asks one.

"What happens if you get shot in the dress?"

I blink a couple times. "Well, I guess I'd get the wound taken care of, take the dress home, wash it, fix it, and put it back on." *What else am I supposed to say to something like that?*

"No, no. I mean, uh . . ." His voice trails off, and he drags a flat hand across his throat. "Like, would you be buried in the dress?"

"I don't know," I answer, laughing. "Hopefully, we won't have to find out."

"Well, I'd come to your funeral just to make sure."

"Thank you. I'm glad to know somebody has my back."

I can't stop laughing. *I hope I don't have to be buried in the dress.* I can't believe I'm halfway done. I feel like maybe, in some small way, I *am* making a difference—at least to those closest to me. This dress has become a huge part of who I am. Though I thoroughly enjoyed the night's celebration, I can't help but wonder what the next half of the year will bring. What I don't know is that in the coming months, I'll find myself feeling shaken, bruised, and beaten. I'm about to learn what happens when you tie your identity to what you do instead of who you are. Like the kids shouting at the deep end, I'm about to cannonball into a pool of darkness. And nothing I've been through could have prepared me for that dive.

July 17, 2012
Day 189

Outfit: black dress, pink polka-dot skirt, white ribbon tie, pink polka-dot hair tie, black flats

The Facts: In the United States, victims of labor trafficking have been found among the nation's migrant and seasonal farmworkers, including adults and children who harvest crops and raise animals.[1]

Total Raised: $4,181.00

One Dress. One Year. For Freedom.

If to be feelingly alive to the sufferings of my fellow-creatures . . . is to be a fanatic, I am one of the most incurable fanatics ever permitted to be at large.

—William Wilberforce[2]

15

Running on Adrenaline

Day 191
Adrenaline Youth Camp

The tangy scent of sunscreen lingers on our skin, and the muggy, salty air presses in on us like a sauna. Daytona Beach in the middle of July is no place for sissies. Only tourists and teenagers brave the sweltering midday heat. Usually they're plunging into the cool waves of the Atlantic. The only thing saving us as we crouch on the beach near the shoreline is the slight breeze coming off the water. Well, that and the fact that we're having a blast. I can already tell that Adrenaline Youth Camp is going to be a highlight of the summer. Every July, some of the same kids who attend Kids-a-Flame Camp and our youth winter retreat swarm the El Caribe Resort for a week. Because we see each other so many times throughout the year, Adrenaline feels like a reunion. Sandwiched between worship services are weeklong competitions, including beach volleyball and Ultimate Frisbee. For those of us who are not inclined to play sports, there's lots of free time for swimming in the pool and ocean.

Because we're on the beach, I'm wearing my swimsuit right now. I can't believe it's Thursday—the last day of camp. I push my hair behind my ear and study the damp sand underneath me. Morgan's head is right next to mine. Water creeps up under our knees and deposits tiny clams onto the sand in front of us. As soon as they settle, they wriggle furiously into the ground.

"What are you doing?" a familiar voice asks.

A shadow covers us. Morgan and I look up. It's Rodney, the youth pastor from nearby Tarpon Springs. He organizes the camp.

"We're watching clams," I say.

"What?" His eyebrow arches.

"These clams." I scoop up a handful of wet sand and water, displaying the tiny clams.

He nods, giving us a weird look. I can only imagine how we appear, both of us kneeling in wet sand with our faces inches from the ground.

"Every time a wave comes in, it brings these little clams," Morgan explains, holding one up.

"We're watching them dig back into the sand. And also cheering for them."

"I see," he says, shaking his head. "I saw you guys from up the beach. You looked funny, so I took a picture. But since you still didn't notice me, I thought I'd come find out what you were doing. Good luck." He leaves us to our clam watching and moves down the beach.

As he walks away, Morgan turns to me. "We should pick our favorites and race them to see which one digs down fastest."

"Okay."

On the count of three, we set two clams next to each other in the wet sand.

We kneel on the beach and yell, "Go! Go! Go! You can do it!"

The clams disappear under the sand at the same time. It's a tie. Another shadow passes in front of us.

"What are you guys doing?"

We look up to see Erin towering over us. At least she isn't looking at us like we're weird—she already knows we are.

"Racing clams! Wanna join us?"

"Yes!"

Now there are three of us kneeling in the sand. We have a few three-way races. Each of us wins two before Erin runs off to join some other friends in the water.

Pushing back on her heels, Morgan wipes damp sand off her knees. Looking up at the position of the sun, she says, "We should go get showers if we want to be ready for the afternoon service."

"Yeah, you're right."

Trudging back up the beach, we laugh at ourselves. As we come up the steps to the hotel courtyard, we see Rodney again. "Did you save all the clams?" he asks.

I give him an exaggerated eye roll. "We weren't *saving* them. We were *watching* them."

"And *racing* them," Morgan adds.

"Oh, really?" he says, rolling his eyes back at me. "Who won?"

"It was a tie."

"Then I think we need a tiebreaker. Go back out on the beach and have another race, then come give me the results."

Morgan and I look at each other.

"Fine," I say, shrugging my shoulders. It doesn't take much to convince us. We set our stuff down and run back out to the beach.

"Best two out of three wins," Morgan says. We have to make sure there's no tie this time.

"Agreed."

Dropping back to our knees, we pick our contestants. I win the first heat. Morgan wins the second. We're down to a tiebreaker race. Our clams dig furiously—desperate to get away from us. When it's over, we rinse off our legs again and carry our clams back to the hotel courtyard.

"So, who won?" Rodney asks, as we come up the stairs.

"I did." I hold up my winning clam. "This is Gilligan."

"And this is Skipper." Morgan holds her clam out. "He's a little pudgy, but everybody loves him."

Rodney laughs. "Glad to hear it."

We head back to the water to set Gilligan and Skipper free and finally make our way back to our hotel room to get ready for the rest of the day. I want to get all the salt and sand off before I have to put on the dress. I look like I'm the one who's been digging in the sand, not Gilligan.

Our last evening service is taking place in the same conference room as the rest of our services, but the room has been transformed. All the chairs have been put away. The lighting is dimmed, and as students pack in, it begins to feel cozy. We're sitting with our small groups on the floor. Groups are divided by rooms, so mine consists of Mom, Erin, Morgan, and Allison. We found a place close to the stage.

Rodney walks to the front.

"Hey, everyone! Can I have your attention up here? I have the awards for the winners of the sports competitions from this week." The room erupts with cheers and whistles.

"Let's start with Ultimate Frisbee!"

As he begins calling names, the cheers only get louder. The winning team from each event comes forward to get their prize pins. Just as Rodney is wrapping up, he pauses.

"I have one more winner to announce. Morgan and Bethany, can you come up here?"

Looking at each other, we stand up and take the few steps to the front.

"We had, uh, an unorthodox sports competition this year."

Morgan and I make eye contact with Erin and try not to laugh.

"While you were all off playing volleyball and Frisbee, I found these two . . ." He pauses, looking at us. "Racing clams."

Our bodies shake as we try to hold in our laughter. He has us introduce ourselves, then says, "This is our official Adrenaline 2012 Clam Race trophy." He pulls out a trinket box made from a clam's shell and hands it to me. "It goes to Bethany Winz and her clam, Gilligan. This is Gilligan's father. He's very proud of his son."

I try my best to put on a serious face. "Thank you," I say.

After a little more banter, he sends us back to our seats. While we were receiving our award, the worship band took their places on stage behind us. Rodney turns to the lead singer.

"Hey, hand me your hat." He pulls it off his head and tosses it to Rodney. Setting it on the edge of the stage, Rodney says, "As we start worship, you guys can bring your offering up here and put it in the hat. Tonight's offering is going to Bethany and her dress project."

During our afternoon session, Rodney brought me to the front and told everyone what I was doing with the dress. He invited them to bring their money tonight and be a part of ending slavery. The band starts to play as he prays to open the service. The rich sounds of bass and guitar fill the conference room.

All 160 of us stand. As we begin worship, I can see the open hat sitting on the stage. My friends and I watch a steady stream of teenagers and adult chaperones make their way forward to drop their offering in it. As they do, the band sings about seeing a generation coming into their own, rising up and living out a selfless faith. The words come to life as each person drops in a bill or a handful of change. I try to sing despite the lump forming in my throat. I'm not alone in this journey. The line inches forward. I'm surrounded by people who care about ending human trafficking, and their compassion is moving them to give. It is a moment I'll need to remember when my own energy for the project plummets over the coming months.

July 30, 2012
Day 202

Outfit: black dress, white shirt, green cardigan, yellow flats

The Facts: When children live in poverty or don't have access to schooling, they are more vulnerable to trafficking.[1]

Amount Raised: $4,865.09

One Dress. One Year. For Freedom.

Just a few weeks ago, International Justice Mission was able to work with local police in the Philippines to rescue young women from exploitation. One of IJM's lawyers talked about what it was like to be part of the operation. Today people are free because of the work that IJM is doing—work that we can partner in by giving.[2]

16

Good Enough?

Day 202
My House, AKA Dress Central

This year I've been living my life on a stage, and the dress has been my costume. Some days that inspires me to do and be more. But lately, knowing that people are watching me sits like a weight on my chest. I want to be perfect so that the people who support me have a reason to be proud. Every day, though, I'm reminded of just how imperfect I am. Take this morning, for example—this hot, humid morning. I feel worn down. No matter how much I blog or tweet or encourage people to give toward ending slavery, the response feels minimal. The excitement of this summer has slipped through my fingers, leaving me frustrated. And the humidity of Florida in August isn't doing anything to help.

I'm out of the shower and dressed, already feeling sweaty and irritable. Flopping down on my bed, I try to sort through the jumble of thoughts in my head. Today's the kind of day where I'm struggling to find the positive. I don't like much about my life right now. I hate that I had to shave my face this morning. Again. I hate the lack of creativity in my outfit combinations. I hate that I'm not putting as much effort into my blog as I should. I hate that I'm so far away from my fund-raising goal. I hate that I'm going into my senior year of high school so unhappy. Have I mentioned that I hate humidity? I do. I scream into my pillow. I sound like a hormonal teenage girl. And that's exactly what I am. In fact, if my blood tests are to be believed, I have enough of some hormones in my body for two people. I would like to give them back to whomever they belong.

On top of the thundering hormones and the general discontent, I hear shame whisper the one thing that scares me more than anything else: "You're not good enough." A tear slips down my cheek. I know all the right answers. I know I'm not defined by what I do. But right now, all I can think about are the times I've failed. When I'm feeling emotionally down, I tend to replay the moments I should have been more, done more, or said something different. They make it easy to believe that I'm hopelessly screwed up. I'll never be able to get my act together. I close my eyes and take a deep breath, wishing I could shake these feelings.

A few weeks ago, on one of his last nights with us, Albert gave the message at youth group. One story he shared was about a friend of his who was facing some really difficult things. When Albert asked him how he was able to handle it, his friend said, "He is good, he is enough, and he will sustain us." These words, which have popped into my head several times since that night, were easy to hear when things were going well, but lately life has been moving in a different direction. *He is good. He is enough. He will sustain me.* I don't feel like this is true. I don't feel like God can sustain me—or if he can, maybe he's just choosing not to. I feel like my body is falling apart, and there's nothing I can do about it. I try to dislodge the despair that's settled in my heart. I'm desperate for some hope. But for now, all I have is a truth that I can't feel.

I push myself up off my bed and wander into the living room. Mom's at her computer. I plop down on the couch. "Can we *please* do something about all this hair?" I swallow, trying not to cry.

She turns her chair to face me. "Of course. I meant to tell you that I started looking at options for laser hair removal."

"Okay. I'm just ready to *do* something about it." I blink back more tears. "I'm so freaking sick of this."

Her voice is soft. "I know. I'll see what we can do about it this week."

Day 205
Laser Hair Removal Center

I lie down, eyes closed, on a long aesthetician's table. Music plays quietly as Sharon, the laser practitioner, moves around the small room. I inhale deeply. Perhaps I should major in deep breathing when I get to college next year. I'm getting pretty good at it. I know the treatment is going to hurt, but I don't care at this point. I'm just ready to get started.

"Okay, Bethany," Sharon says. I open my eyes and look at her. The laser machine makes a dull, thumping noise beside me. "We're almost ready. First, I need you to put on these attractive glasses." She smiles, handing me a pair of amber-tinted, wrap-around sunglasses.

I laugh and slide them on. The entire world is yellow.

"They'll help protect your eyes from the lasers," she explains. "Are you ready to get started?"

I nod.

"Try to relax." I close my eyes as she brings the laser, which is attached to the thumping machine by a long cord, close to my face. When it touches my skin, it feels like the snap of a rubber band. This is the first of many regular treatments I'll have with

Sharon. I'm grateful that I've finally found someone who can do something about this hair. I just hope it actually works. I'm ready to be done worrying about it. So many things have led me here. I hope Albert's right about God being able to sustain me. I have a feeling that this is only the beginning.

This visit is a good first step in my healing process, but now I'm struggling with so much more than excess facial hair. My yearlong journey in the dress is uncovering layer upon layer of issues, including my struggle with perfectionism, my desire to attach my self-worth to how well I perform, my feelings of unworthiness, the shame of not being the person I think I should be, and my inability to feel comfortable in my own skin. Each issue bears its own smothering weight, and they are all pressing down on me at once.

Fall becomes a season of unexplainable darkness and discouragement. Maybe there's some spiritual reason for it, but at the moment, it just feels to me like I'm a failure. I'm trapped in a cycle of accepting lies about who I am and who I can become. I believe in freedom from slavery for others. I'm just not sure I'll ever find freedom for myself—freedom from self-loathing, freedom from being a people-pleaser, freedom from the sense that I'm not good enough and never will be. It's going to take more than a couple laser treatments to set me free.

August 19, 2012
Day 222

Outfit: black dress, blue scarf/shawl, black belt, yellow flats

The Facts: There are an estimated 600,000–800,000 men, women, and children trafficked across international borders annually.[1]

Amount Raised: $4,903.09

One Dress. One Year. For Freedom.

Yesterday was one of those days where my fragile illusion of control shattered into a million pieces, and now I don't quite know what my next step should be. I know that the God I worship is far bigger than the circumstances I face, but rarely do I live like I believe it.

According to Louie Giglio, "We worship God, not simply with words about how big he is, but by the confidence we show in his bigness."[2]

So today, Sabbath, a day of rest and worship, I choose to trust. I choose to rest. I choose to worship. He is big. I am not. He is wise. I am not. He is in control. I am not. So why do I work and worry so much? Why do I insist on carrying such a heavy burden when he says his yoke is easy, his burden light? This verse has been coming to mind a lot lately: "Cast all your anxiety on him because he cares for you" (1 Pet. 5:7).

The control I cling to is a burden I was never meant to carry. So today, I choose to lay my anxiety down at the foot of the cross and rest in the fact that my Shepherd is carrying me. What burdens do you need to leave at his feet today?

17

An Unexpected Gift

Day 242
The Driveway

The Saturday sun bakes our driveway into a strip of molten lava. Welcome to September in Florida. The weather doesn't really start to cool down until late October. Heat seeps through the soles of my feet as I walk down to the mailbox. After pulling it open, I grab the mail and thumb through it. Under the letters and fliers, there's a small padded envelope addressed to me. I love mail. I walk back inside the house. The roar of a happy crowd fills the adjoining room as the college team on the television scores a touchdown. Dad groans. It could be a long game.

I sit down at the kitchen table and slide my finger under the seal of the package. I shake it, and a gauzy red pouch slides into my hand. Inside is a necklace. It's a simple gold key attached to a chain. On the key, one word is engraved: *freedom*. Sometimes I get emails from people who ask for my address so they can send me things to wear with the dress. This package is from a woman who wrote to me in August.

The note inside the package explains that the necklace is a Giving Key. The Giving Keys program hires people transitioning out of homelessness to engrave recycled keys with an inspirational word. The keys are then sold. Each key is designed to be worn until the owner has embraced whatever word is on their key. Then they pass it on to someone who needs the message more than they do.

The woman who sent me the key has picked the word *freedom* for me because of my focus on ending human trafficking. She also tells me that this key is a reminder of God's grace. Grace is something I could use right now. I don't seem to have a whole lot of it for myself. I pick up the necklace, rubbing the word with my thumb. *What does grace really mean for me right now? Does God still have grace for me even though nothing is turning out the way I thought it would?* Her note about restoration and love is like water to my parched heart. She doesn't know half of what I'm struggling with, but her words are ones I need to hear. I finish reading the letter with a thousand thoughts tumbling through my mind.

I fold it and slip it back inside the envelope. She's right. The whole reason behind this project is that I am working to free people from trafficking. But what I've been finding is that I, too, am in desperate need of freedom. Picking up the necklace, I loop it around my neck and fasten the clasp in place. Dad cheers along with the television.

As I walk to my room, I hope her words of grace will sink into my soul. I'm going to need them tomorrow when I speak about the dress at another youth group gathering. I'm still struggling with how The Dress Project is going. I want to believe that what I'm doing matters. I want to believe that God can use people like me and like the teenagers I'm getting ready to talk to, but right now I wonder if I'm doing any good. I want to believe that God is working in and through me, even though I can't see it or feel it happening. I need God's grace to meet me in the middle of my doubts and fears. I just hope I'm able to encourage the kids I am going to meet tomorrow despite my own struggles.

Day 243
Spring of Life United Methodist Church

A few months ago I asked Jarrod if any of the youth pastors he knows would be willing to let me share my story with their youth groups. He connected me with Aaron, the youth pastor at Spring of Life United Methodist Church. When we started planning a time for me to come speak at Spring of Life, I was excited. It used to be that any opportunity to talk about the dress was a positive thing. But now, I don't know. I used to be confident in the dress and its status as a powerful symbol in the fight for freedom. These days, though, I feel ambivalent and anxious. I can't help but question my own motives. Maybe I'm doing this simply to make people think I'm better than others my age.

Tonight I'm supposed to encourage a room full of teenagers to make a difference, but deep down in my soul I feel like a fraud. *How am I going to ask them to do something I can't? How am I going to get up in front of all these kids and say, "I'm doing this dress project because I'm fighting for freedom," when I really want to say, "I'm not so sure I should have done this dress project to begin with."* I feel like I've hit a new low, and I can't stop the negative thoughts from bombarding my brain. *If I can't clean up this emotional mess in order to share my project with the Spring of Life group, then I may as well give up now. Right?* Despite my anxieties, I'm going through with it. I made a commitment and can't back out now.

So here I am, riding to the church with Mom. My notes are in my lap. I lean against the van door. The sun is setting as she pulls into the parking lot. I don't really want to put myself out there tonight. I don't want to meet new people or go through the motions of acting like I'm excited about what I'm doing. I know my emotions can lie, but right now they're the only voice I can hear.

"Bethany?"

"Hmm?"

"Are you ready?" Mom turns the van off.

"Yeah." I sigh.

"Are you okay?"

"I don't know. I'm just having a hard time right now. Nothing is turning out the way I thought it would. Not with the dress. Not with raising money. Not with me. So getting up in front of a bunch of kids to talk about it is . . . I don't know . . . it's hard."

Mom doesn't answer right away.

"I know this year has been difficult in a lot of ways." She pauses. "But I also know that you do a great job talking about the dress. Even if you can't see it or feel it, what you are doing is making a difference. And kids need to hear what you have to say about slavery and freedom. We all do. Tonight is going to be good."

Half my mouth turns up in a smile. It's how I feel right now—halfhearted. My well of energy and passion is running low.

"Thanks. I guess I'm as ready as I'll ever be."

"I love you."

"I love you too, Mom. Thanks for coming with me."

As I open the car door, the humidity engulfs me. I'm doing this. I said I would, and so I am. Mom and I walk up to the building. I could use a little of the grace and freedom I'm going to talk about tonight.

Two hundred and forty-three days down. I pull open the glass door and step into the coolness of the church sanctuary. Only 123 days left to go. Right now I'm no longer drawing on emotion or passion to keep me going. I'm stubborn. I made a commitment, and I'm going to see it through—even though I don't want to, and even though I don't feel like I have anything left to say. Maybe this is what growing up feels like—pushing forward even when you're not sure where you're going.

September 17, 2012
Day 251

Outfit: black dress, royal blue shirt, blue-striped blouse, black heels

The Facts: Approximately 80 percent of human trafficking victims are women and girls, and up to 50 percent are minors.[1]

Amount Raised: $5,176.09

One Dress. One Year. For Freedom.

In India, many people become enslaved because of poverty and a lack of job opportunities. That's why Not for Sale has partnered with Open Hand to provide jobs to people who are at risk or are survivors of trafficking.[2]

Women from local shelters and vocational programs are recruited for the Not for Sale training program and appointed a social worker. As part of the program, they are offered counseling, child care services, literacy training, savings and financial guidance, and further transferable job skills instruction.

To those of you who have donated, thank you for helping make this happen. If you'd like to get involved, I encourage you to give. Be sure to let me know so that we can get your donation added to the total!

18

The Day I Dyed

Day 268
My Room

My flexible homeschooling schedule has been great this year. After I get my work done, the rest of the day is mine. If something important comes up, I can take care of it. Today, the important thing I need to take care of is the dress. The dress has issues. I'm halfway through my homework for Valencia, but it's only Thursday. I don't have class again until Monday, so I'll just finish it later this weekend. Right now, the dress is more pressing.

Standing in the middle of my room, I study myself in my mirrored closet doors. My hair is out of control. Again. Bending forward, I gather my unruly curls on top of my head and twist them into a bun. Curls escape in every direction, so the finished style is messy at best. Smoothing my crown of frizz is a daunting task. Some days I win. Some days my hair wins. Today, my hair is winning.

Right now the dress is also winning, or losing, depending on which way you look at it. Putting my hands on my hips, I look into the mirror again. The hair is doable. The dress? Not so much.

I pull off my pink garage-sale blazer and the cute sea-green shirt Erin loaned me, dropping them on my desk. Blazer and cardigan outfits have become my favorites. They're easy to put together, but they still look cute.

As I work my way down the buttons, I can feel how worn the dress is after 268 days. The fabric is smooth and waxy beneath my fingers. The black cotton is wearing thin. The outer layer of the skirt has shrunk, but the nylon lining hasn't shrunk with it. There's a giant crease in the lining along the bottom of the dress, so the skirt balloons out. By now, though, the hem isn't where the problems stop. Nobody can tell from the outside, but the entire lining is pilled, worn, stretched, and nearly ripped.

The evening light flooding the room behind me frames my reflection like a halo. Angelic is not the term I would use to describe myself though. Maybe ragamuffin couture? Threadbare chic? The dress has been a trooper, but it definitely needs a minor makeover. I shrug it off and toss it over my desk chair. After throwing on a pair of yoga pants and a T-shirt, I get to work.

I grab the iron and the ironing board from my parents' closet. Dragging them into my room, I set the iron down and unfold the board and stretch out the dress on the board's flat surface. The iron gives off a little puff of steam, hissing and sighing. Maybe I can make the dress look a little more put together if I iron out the giant crease on the hem. As I touch the iron to the dress, I feel a tug as I try to move it down the hemline. Lifting the iron, I see strings of black, melted plastic attaching it to the dress. My stomach ties itself in a knot. Of course. The lining is nylon. You don't iron nylon. Ever. Unless you like to burn things. Even though the iron is on low, it immediately melted the lining. All it left in its wake is a gaping hole.

I collapse onto my bed. All my ideas for improving the dress quickly become lost in questions about how I'm going to fix the mess I've just made. I bury my head in my hands and sigh. *Why am I so stupid?* After a few minutes of stewing in frustration, I reassess the damage. I pull at the hole to see how big it actually is. Because it's in the lining, I could still wear it. Nobody would really know how messed up things were on the inside—nobody but me. But the whole thing probably needs to be replaced.

I open my closet to look for my craft stash. Sorting through random scraps of fabric from other projects, I eventually find the rest of the black fabric I used to make the dress. I was supposed to use this fabric to make the second dress. I don't have extra lining material, so this will have to do. I grab it and a pair of scissors.

"There's only one way to do this," I mutter, taking a deep breath. Sometimes I have to talk myself through things. I cut the lining away from the skirt. The fabric shifts on the ironing board with every snip. "Maybe I can figure out a way to replace the lining." After examining the way I constructed the dress, I realize that I won't be able to simply replace the lining. I plop back down on the bed. Maybe I can crawl back under the covers and get a redo on today. I'm already tired of sewing, and I haven't even started yet. *Is this even worth it? What if I just gave up now and didn't wear the dress tomorrow?*

I push the thoughts away as soon as they pop into my head, ashamed that I would even consider them. But still, it would be so much easier to just give up. Before I can think too much about what it would be like to slide into a pair of jeans, I pull myself up, step back to the ironing board and dress, and cut it just below the waistline. I'm going to replace the entire skirt. It's the only way to fix it.

Once the two pieces of the dress are separated, I take them out to the living room and spread them out on the giant rug.

Spreading the skirt across the new material, I cut around it. Sitting back on my heels, I sigh. Sewing isn't my forte. I discovered that when I first made the dress. But I have to finish this, one way or another.

Standing up, I walk to the kitchen for a drink.

"How's it going?" Mom asks from the stove. The smell of garlic and tomatoes makes my stomach growl—spaghetti for dinner.

"Well." I hesitate. "I have to replace the entire skirt."

"Really?" she asks.

"Yep." I shrug.

"Well, good luck. Dad should be home before too long, so I'll call you when dinner is ready."

"Thanks, Mom." I return to the living room and the dress. I spend at least an hour nipping, tucking, and pinning, trying to get it just right. Once it's pinned, I take it back to my sewing machine in my bedroom. Feeding the fabric under the needle, I sew the new skirt pieces together. The new cotton fabric is looking much better than the old, frayed nylon. Pinning the new skirt to the bodice, I put the dress back together. Now for the buttonholes—and since I only replaced the skirt, the top ones are still intact. Six buttonholes and a spaghetti dinner later, I'm done.

Although I'm ready to collapse on the floor, instead I try on the dress. I twirl around in front of my mirror, smoothing down the skirt. It flares a little more than it used to, but I like it. I head back out to the kitchen to show Mom, who is finishing up the dishes. "Well, what do you think?"

Looking up from the sink, she surveys me and the new dress.

"It looks great. Nice job," she says, smiling.

"Thanks." I twirl around again. It feels good to finally get something right—well, mostly right. The one problem with replacing the skirt after 268 days of wear is that the new material is much darker than the old. Maybe I'll try to dye the faded top of the dress. That's a battle for tomorrow though.

Day 269
Dye Workshop

Friday dawns with one purpose: dye the dress. Once the dress is done, I will be threadbare chic no more. I feel like a designer getting ready to work her magic. I just hope this works. Armed with one bottle of dye, one large pot, and my half new, half old dress, I set up shop in the kitchen. I can hear Mom working in the other room. Morning sunshine streams through the garden window as I stir the bottle of dye into the pot of water. The black dye bubbles and spits, rising up the sides of the stainless steel pot. I turn off the heat. What I don't want to do is light the dress on fire, dye my hands, or alter the dress in any unintended way. It would be just like me to do something weird to the dress and still have to wear it for three months. I push the fabric down into the pot with a spoon, following the instructions on the dye bottle to the letter. I even dye the whole dress a second time in the washing machine with a packet of powder dye.

I hang the dress to dry in the laundry room. I can already tell that the top is still lighter than the skirt. If I was looking for perfect, this isn't it. Still, it's better than it was.

A few hours later, the dress is finally dry. I lift it off the hanger and head back to my room to try it on. Mom calls down the hall, "Bethany, can you make sure you clean the washer?"

"Yeah," I call back. "Just a minute."

Dyeing all the other clothes in the house black is also not part of the plan. It's a good thing Mom reminded me to clean up after myself. Once I'm back in the dress, I walk across the house to the laundry room. As I pull the bleach off the shelf, I remind myself to be careful. Bleach and a black dress won't mix well. I pour a little bit into the washer and start a new cycle. Mission accomplished.

A few minutes later, I look down at the dress. There are two pink-red splotches on the front. *Where on earth did those come from*? I try to rub them away, but they won't come off.

Then it hits me.

The bleach. I spilled bleach on my dress. And of course I spilled it on the part I just replaced. Some days I wonder if I'm living in a sitcom. Despite all my best efforts, I've done something weird to the dress.

I should be crying, but instead, I giggle. It feels good to laugh a little, especially after these long weeks of sadness. I wish the whole skirt was still black, but for some reason, I'm okay that it's not. Maybe I'm finally starting to understand how little I can control. No matter how hard I try, I just can't manage every little detail. Perhaps I'm learning to enjoy life, even with all of its craziness. It takes me a few weeks to figure out how to cover up the blotches on the dress with a fabric marker—after all, I still want it to be presentable for the rest of the year. But if anyone looks closely, they'll see the spots. The dress isn't perfect, and neither am I. Maybe if I can embrace that, then I'll find a little more freedom myself.

October 25, 2012
Day 289

Outfit: black dress, white top, black sweater, silver sandals, black dangle earrings

The Facts: The Global Slavery Index estimates that in 2014, there were 35.8 million people enslaved around the world.[1]

Amount Raised: $5,444.09

One Dress. One Year. For Freedom.

This week, International Justice Mission is opening their sixteenth field office—IJM Gulu. This office will allow staff members to help families fighting property grabbing and other forms of injustice. You can find out more on their website.[2]

19

Denim, Diamonds, and Desserts

Day 312
Winter Park Farmers Market

Soft light illuminates rough brick walls inside the farmers market. Round tables draped with crisp, white tablecloths and topped with floral arrangements line the room. People are milling around a dessert table filled with every kind of sweet imaginable. Crystals twinkle on the tables. Sodas in hand, Erin, Morgan, and I take it all in. Stepping into the old train station turned farmers market is like stepping into a birthday wonderland.

Tonight is Mrs. Kim's Denim, Diamonds, and Desserts Party to celebrate her fiftieth birthday. In lieu of birthday presents, Mrs. Kim, who's a good friend of my family, has asked her friends to donate to Restore International in honor of The Dress Project. I still can't believe she has asked. She's also asked Erin, Morgan, and me to provide the entertainment for the evening. We're dancing to one of my favorite songs, "You Are More" by Tenth Avenue North. It's a piece we performed in church a few weeks ago, and Mrs. Kim liked it enough that she asked us to do it again tonight.

For now, the three of us are enjoying a few minutes of quiet at our table before we perform.

"This place looks amazing," Erin says, looking around.

"It really does," Morgan agrees.

"I'm just looking forward to eating a piece of that chocolate cake after we dance," I say, eyeing the desserts piled on a row of tables across the room. Some are store bought, but many were made and brought by guests.

My friends laugh at me. "I want to try it all," Erin says. "How are we supposed to pick?"

We all like to bake, so this is our kind of party. Baked goods feed our bodies and our souls. We even brought carrot cake balls—the treat Morgan and I swore we would never make again—as our contribution to the dessert table. They were just as difficult to make and delicious to eat as last time. Everywhere I look, people are wearing denim and bling. There are jeans, jean skirts, jean jackets, diamonds, and fake diamonds. I have a jean jacket to wear with the dress after I perform, but denim doesn't lend itself to dancing, so for now Erin, Morgan, and I are wearing matching red dresses and sticking out like sore thumbs. It feels weird to be out of the black dress.

My phone vibrates in my hand. It's Bob Goff. I called him earlier today with some questions about the home Restore International runs for trafficking survivors. I want to share an update at the party about what they're doing. I also might have wanted an excuse to talk to Bob.

"I have to run outside and take this. Come get me when we're on."

"Will do," Erin says.

I slip out the door and onto the front patio. The air is crisp. November has ushered in some cooler weather, and I am thankful.

"Hello?"

"Bethany? It's Bob!"

"Hi, Bob! Thanks so much for calling me back." I'm already smiling. Bob's excitement for life is infectious. He tells me about what Restore has been up to and gives me the latest on the safe home for survivors of trafficking, a newer venture that I'd only seen mentioned online in passing. I'm still smiling when Erin taps my shoulder and waves me back in.

"Bob, thanks again for calling." We wrap up our conversation.

As soon as I hit "end," Erin grabs me by the elbow. "We're on," she says, pulling me inside. We work our way through the tables. I set down my phone, and the three of us take our places as Mrs. Kim introduces us.

"I have asked these girls to perform the dance they did in church a few weeks ago. It was so beautiful and powerful. Please welcome Erin, Morgan, and Bethany."

Applause fills the room, and the music begins to play. My heart thumps with anticipation. I still love to dance. I love the feeling of using my body to tell a story. Arms extended, I think about each movement. Erin and Morgan move in tandem with me. We've practiced these motions a hundred times. I lose myself in the song and start to wonder, *What if I could really believe that the things I do don't define who I am?* As we move together, my mind sinks into that thought.

I want to believe that. I need to believe that. It's been two long months of struggling with these dark feelings. This fight against shame—the voice that is constantly telling me that I am not enough—has been eating away at me. My goals in wearing the dress revolve around wanting to be good and wanting to do good. But the year is almost over, and I don't know how much good I've done. I still struggle with my perfectionistic ideals and feel inadequate when I don't measure up to them. I still want people to notice me and what I'm doing. I still work hard to make my life mean something. I know Jesus died to redeem me, but it's difficult to believe that when I don't see any changes in myself, when there is so much I still don't like about myself. I feel like I've failed in so many ways this year. I can't help but wonder how The Dress

Project would have been better had I put a little more effort into it. Yet here we are, dancing to a song that reminds me that God's love for me has nothing to do with what I've done, good or bad. He loves me. Just as I am. Maybe that's what he's been trying to teach me all along.

As the music fades and our dance comes to an end, the room erupts in applause. Mrs. Kim addresses the crowd again.

"Most of you know that I've asked you to donate to Bethany's dress project for my birthday. She's going to share more details about her journey in a few minutes, but thank you in advance for your gifts." The three of us run to the bathroom to change. I put the black dress back on. I cannot wait to tell the partygoers about Restore International.

I love that Mrs. Kim asked me to be part of her celebration. More than that, I love that she wants to be part of ending slavery. The last few months have been hard, but I'm starting to feel a little light breaking through the darkness. Today has been a bright spot for sure. It's been good to enjoy the things and people I love: dancing, desserts, Erin, Morgan, Tenth Avenue North, an encouraging call with Bob, and others sharing my passion and donating to Restore. It's as if Jesus is reminding me one more time that he loves me and hasn't forgotten me. Through the highs and lows and joys and disappointments of this year, he's been here—even when I couldn't see or feel him.

I have six weeks left in the dress, and I feel a little peace moving into my heart. God isn't done with me yet. He's still making me into the person he wants me to be. My thoughts, my dreams, my hopes—he's changing all of me.

December 23, 2012
Day 348

Outfit: black dress, white sweater, silver sandals, silver cuff, silver layered necklace, hoop earrings

The Facts: International Justice Mission works in 20 communities in Africa, Latin America, South and Southeast Asia. They have trained more than 13,000 officials and officers in the fight against trafficking and have won more than 770 convictions against human traffickers.[1]

Amount Raised: $6,677.09

One Dress. One Year. For Freedom.

Today I was going to post something deep and meaningful about Christmas, but I feel like I can hardly put two coherent thoughts together. I'm tired, I'm frustrated, and I need to be reminded yet again of Christ, who came in the midst of chaos and confusion to bring me back to himself. He who gave me life, who caused the death of death itself. I love Josh Wilson's song "Jesus is Alive." It reminds us that hope is here because Jesus is alive.

That is the real truth of Christmas.

PS: The dress and I get to see Josh sing this live at a concert tonight!

20

Hanging It Up

Day 366
My Bedroom

I twirl one last time in front of the mirror, surveying the black dress in all its glory and with all its flaws. It's been through a lot this year, and the worn buttonholes and faded bodice tell the tale. My blinds are shut tight against the darkness. It's hard to believe that it's almost 11 p.m. on January 10, 2013. Today was my last day wearing the dress. It seems right that it's ending in the same room where it started 366 days ago. It's been 366 days of the dress. It's been 366 different ways of wearing it without buying anything new to go with it. It's been 366 days of trying to be better than I have ever been and doing more than I have ever done before. Last night I scheduled my last outfit post of the year. I included a video of all 366 days. As I watched it, I found myself laughing at some of the outfits I came up with. Creative? Yes. Different? Yes. Desperate to find something to wear? Almost every night. I gave my blog post one last read through before I scheduled it to go live this morning.

January 10, 2013
Day 366

Outfit: black dress, cream cardigan with sequin trim, silver layered necklace, black flats

The Facts: Human trafficking is tied with arms dealing as the second largest criminal industry in the world. Men, women, and children are sold into a $150 billion annual market for sex and labor.[1]

Amount Raised: $8,615.09

One Dress. One Year. For Freedom.

Day 366, and I don't even know where to begin. What a year it's been. It's been 366 days of the same dress and 366 different ways of wearing that dress. Some outfits I would wear again in a heartbeat, others I most definitely would not. Each day was an adventure, an adventure that wouldn't have been possible without a whole posse on board. They're the people who have lent or donated clothes, taken pictures, helped me come up with outfit ideas, prayed for me, and cheered me on every step of the way. And I'm so, so grateful.

I'm also really grateful for you. To each of you who have read the blog or left an encouraging note, thank you. And to those of you who have donated, you're making a difference. You are setting people free.

I started the year with a goal of raising $100,000. A few weeks ago, as I faced the unlikelihood of meeting that goal, I decided to shoot for $10,000 instead. And yes, I would be thrilled if we got there, but right now, I'm grateful for every single dollar that every single one of you has given. And it goes so far beyond the dollar amount. Lives are being changed, stories are being rewritten. That's amazing. Thank you.

Most of all, the thanks for this entire year goes to Jesus. He has made it all possible. He demonstrated for us what it means to love the poor and the oppressed, and I'm grateful that he's allowed us to share his heart for them.

And this video is my project recap—all 366 outfits plus fundraising progress throughout the year. The songs are "I Refuse" by Josh Wilson and "The Solution" by Eddie Kirkland.

I wonder who will see the video. I hope it moves people to donate. More than that, I hope it gives them the courage to do what God's calling them to do with a dress or a dream or whatever talent they may possess. Maybe my dream will inspire someone else's dream, just like Elaini's inspired mine. Alone, no one's efforts will amount to much, but together we can break through the darkness of slavery. And somehow, as we work toward this goal, we find this dream shaping us and setting us free.

This black dress has changed me. I rub the bleach spots on the front of the skirt. Neither one of us has come out of the year unscathed. I've learned things about myself that I never knew before. It turns out that The Dress Project wasn't just another overly ambitious idea. It's one I've seen through to the end. I've worn the dress faithfully for an entire year. It's reminded me how much my family loves me. My parents have worked around my schedule, driven me places, and been there to encourage me when I've needed it most. It's shown me again that my friends—especially the ones who loaned me parts of their closets for the year—are some of the very best. They've loved me through the joy, frustration, and darkness.

Tonight, Mom and Dad took me out for frozen yogurt to celebrate the end of the year. We talked about the highlights, including launching my own website, blogging every day, chatting with Bob Goff, connecting with anti-trafficking organizations, raising more than $8,000, sharing my mission with various groups, meeting The Museum and Josh Wilson, and the list could go on and on. The coolest thing about meeting Josh after his concert was that he'd already seen my video of the first part of the project, in which I used his song "I Refuse" as the background music. Somewhere along the way, the dress took on a life of its own.

Of course, the year hasn't been all high points. Some of the hardest days of my life happened while I was wearing the dress. The most frustrating ones occurred before the project even started when I was trying to sew the dress. I doubt I'll ever attempt a sewing project this big again. The saddest day was definitely Day 100. Coming to terms with my overly hormonal body is a journey I'm still on. Just this morning, I had another laser hair removal appointment. Each treatment moves me further from the despair of Day 100, but there's still so much I don't understand about what's going on inside of me, both physically and spiritually. My emotional downward spiral in August wasn't something I had expected. For months, I had felt consumed by feelings of doubt and failure. I couldn't untie the knot in my stomach. It's a new year though, and I finally feel like I'm coming out of it. The darkness is easing up. I can see the light at the end of the dress tunnel. When I chose to wear the dress this year, I didn't know how desperate I was to be free or how the dress would bring those feelings to the surface. The dress was, however, something I chose. People who have been trafficked don't choose the reality they face every day. No one should have to live in that kind of darkness—ever.

It's so weird. Tonight is the last night I'll wear the dress. I won't have to plan my outfits or think about what to write about on my blog. I won't have to ask my friends if I can borrow their clothes or explain to strangers why "I'm wearing the same dress every day," and "No, I don't wear it to bed," and "Yes, I do take it off and wash it. Would you like to smell it?" I won't have to make sure I smooth out the dress under me every time I sit down. I won't have to sit in a ladylike fashion unless I want to. The Dress Project is over.

This weekend, Erin, Morgan, and I are going to hit the thrift stores for a few hours. I can't wait. I'm already planning what I want to buy: cardigans, belts, shoes. I can't wait to wear jeans again. At the same time, I can't imagine waking up tomorrow and not putting the dress on. It's become a part of me. A faded, bedraggled part of me. And it has defined me. Some days, it was a badge of honor. Other days, I could hardly stand it. After a year of wearing it, I know who I am in the dress. It's given me a sense of identity. Tomorrow that identity will be out the window. Who will I be in jeans and a T-shirt? Who will I be wearing clothes that make absolutely no statement at all? I'm ready to find out.

"All right. Here we go."

You know it's time to stop wearing an article of clothing when you start talking to it like it's a person. I work my way down the buttons for the last time. The dress slides to the floor, and I grab sweatpants and a T-shirt. Picking it up, I lay the dress across my desk. It's been through so much. Maybe I should frame it or make a quilt out of it. On second thought, no quilt. That would involve too much sewing. I'm done with sewing for a while. I'll probably just hang it in the closet for now. I'm not quite ready to put it away for good.

As I hang up the dress, I let out one last sigh. This dress is something God has used to show me who he is. In the darkest days, he reminded me that he loves me not because of what I wear or what I talk about or what organization I raise money for. He loves me because I am his. He's given me these passions, but they don't define me. It's probably going to take me a long time to fully understand that though.

I button up the dress on the hanger. I'm so grateful for this past year and all the people who partnered with me. Despite my mixed motives and the months of darkness, wearing the dress made more people aware that slavery exists—and I was able to be part of watching people come together and raise money to help end it.

I pull down my green T-shirt from a nearby hanger. I'm going to wear it with jeans tomorrow. It's the one The Museum signed all those months ago. Across the front it reads, "This Shirt Frees Slaves." I guess I'm not quite ready to quit making a statement with the clothes I wear. I still want the way I live to help bring freedom to men, women, and children around the world. After all, if ordinary people don't do something, who will? Every single one of us is made in God's image—made to be free. Even me. I step back, taking one last look at the dress. This green T-shirt might help free slaves, but it's not alone in the fight. So does my black dress.

One Dress. One Year. For Freedom.

Conclusion

The Journey Continues

Day 800+
Sighişoara, Romania

Sometimes God turns our whole world upside down in an instant. Other times he does it slowly. That's how it happened during the year of the dress. There isn't a moment I can point to when everything changed, but by the end of the year, I saw the whole world in a different way. That's also what happened when I moved to Nashville, Tennessee, to go to college.

Two hundred and twenty-five days after I took off the dress for the last time, I dragged all my belongings up a narrow stairwell and into my first dorm room. I have chosen to major in social justice at Trevecca Nazarene University. It is an opportunity to study the very things I am so passionate about. At sixteen, I started the year with a dress, a blog, and a mission: change the world. That mission and those dreams led me to Trevecca and made me the person I am today, but as I have continued to grow and change, the struggle to establish my identity and what it means to seek justice has grown and changed with me.

I now realize that taking a stand for justice doesn't have to involve a big, dramatic gesture intended to change the entire world. Maybe it's something much smaller—righting wrongs one relationship at a time. I've found that discovering who I am has much less to do with impressing people and much more to do with living a life of faithfulness wherever God has placed me. In high school, that meant wearing the same dress for a year. But in college, it looks different.

The Dress Project has come full circle this summer after my freshman year, and I find myself standing on the balcony of an Orthodox cathedral in Sighişoara, Romania, with a group of fellow Trevecca students. We're a week into our trip to Eastern Europe. Our purpose for this trip isn't to volunteer, but to learn. We're visiting churches, ministries, villages, and cities, learning about what God is doing among his people in this part of the world. We're discovering what it means to serve a God who has a heart for vulnerable people. One of our professors has challenged us to not simply hear the stories of the people we meet as the stories of those who are different from us. He's asked us to think about what it means for us to be vulnerable. That's what I'm thinking about as I stand in the cathedral with my classmates.

The vaulted ceiling soars above us in a wide arc. Sunlight pours in through the windows, illuminating the icons that cover every inch of wall. I lean over the railing, watching the service unfold below us. Rows of wooden chairs crisscross the marble floors in front of a tall lectern. A priest in robes reads Scripture. Even though I can't understand what he's saying, his voice fills the space, echoing up into the balcony. I lean against the cathedral wall, close my eyes for a moment, and breathe in the incense. The whispers of my classmates mingle with the rhythmic sounds of the liturgy. I open my eyes again and look across the church to the other balcony and the two images of Jesus painted on the ceiling above. In one, Jesus reaches down to a dead girl and takes her by the hand, raising her from her bed. In the other, he stretches out his hand and touches the oozing skin of a man with leprosy.

I brush a tear from my cheek and feel the soft skin beneath my fingers. Most of the hair covering my face is light and fine, but it isn't hard to remember when it was dark and coarse. Some days, it still is. From time to time, I still have to shave it. The tears fall faster as I think about all the things in my body that are broken and out of balance. It's good to know that Jesus is still in the business of healing the wounded. I've come a long way in understanding how to live in a broken body, but I'm still bitter that I have to deal with it at all. I just wish Jesus would take it away—that he would reach out and touch me like he touched the leper and leave me with a body that functions like it's supposed to. If there's one thing that makes me feel vulnerable, this is it.

Earlier this week in a different part of Eastern Europe, we spent an afternoon with a few girls who are survivors of trafficking. We visited together, ate pizza, and played games. We also spent some time singing together. As we did, I looked at the faces around me—those of my classmates and of the girls we were visiting—and saw life and beauty. Before we left, they chose one last song. It was a song of blessing and joy and worship, and it was one that we all knew. Languages swirled together as we sang. Many of us heard the words differently that afternoon. How do you worship in the midst of pain? That's a question I still don't know how to answer.

The sound of voices raised in song rings through the cathedral. Worship in the midst of pain. That thought brings fresh tears to my eyes as I look one more time at the picture of Jesus raising the girl from the dead. He's always reached out and touched people in their suffering. Perhaps my pain isn't a curse but a way to begin to understand others. Maybe because of what I've experienced, I can understand in some small way the unspeakable joy of being touched by Jesus, even when he doesn't take the pain away like I often want him to.

I'm still on this journey of learning who I am and who God is. I'm still learning what it means to be his. During my freshman year, the pastor of the church I was attending in Nashville said that we all ask ourselves the same two questions: Am I lovable? Am I valuable? He said we get obsessed with the idea of leaving a legacy because we think that's what gives our lives value when, in reality, our only legacy is that we are loved by God. Even when we can't see what God's doing, he weaves every moment—including the ugly and painful ones—into something beautiful.

This moment in Sighişoara is one of many that God has used to remind me that I am loved. I am free. There will be many more moments in my journey in which God will remind me again, and I'll need every one of them. Your moment may take place at a truck stop in Mobile, Alabama, or at a youth camp in San Francisco, California. You may never wear a dress for a year or struggle with body issues or fly halfway around the world to hear one more time that God is with you in your pain. But you have a powerful legacy. Your truth is the same as mine. God loves you dearly. It may take years to understand it, but it's the only truth that matters. And the craziest part is that when you truly believe it, you start to find freedom.

Notes

Chapter 2 Why Didn't You Come Sooner?

1. "Human Trafficking," the A21 Campaign, accessed June 2, 2015, http://www.thea21campaign.org/content/human-trafficking/gl0ryw.

2. "ILO Says Forced Labour Generates Annual Profits of US$ 150 Billion," International Labour Organization, May 20, 2014, http://www.ilo.org/global/about-the-ilo/newsroom/news/WCMS_243201/lang--en/index.htm.

3. US Department of State, Trafficking in Persons Report June 2014, "Introductory Material," 9, accessed July 16, 2015, http://www.state.gov/documents/organization/226844.pdf.

Chapter 3 Going Public

1. Made in a Free World, "Slavery Footprint Survey," Slavery Footprint, accessed June 2, 2015, http://slaveryfootprint.org/survey/#where_do_you_live.

2. "Child Labor Facts," Compassion International, accessed June 2, 2015, http://www.compassion.com/child-advocacy/find-your-voice/quick-facts/child-labor-quick-facts.htm.

Chapter 4 Camping in the Dress

1. "What We Do," Restore International, accessed June 2, 2015, http://restoreinternational.org/what-we-do/.

Chapter 5 Cutting Out the Middleman

1. "Human Trafficking," the A21 Campaign, accessed June 2, 2015, http://www.thea21campaign.org/content/human-trafficking/gl0ryw.

Chapter 6 A Heart-Breaking Party

1. Rob Morris, Love146, accessed June 2, 2015, http://love146.org/love-story/.

2. "Slavery," Love146, accessed June 2, 2015, http://love146.org/slavery/.

3. William Wilberforce, quoted in "Modern Day Slavery–Never Again Say You Did Not Know!" *Christian Today*, March 5, 2007, http://www.christiantoday.com/article/modern.day.slavery.never.again.say.you.did.not.know/9778.htm.

Chapter 7 Not for Sale

1. "Child Trafficking in the US," UNICEF, accessed July 2, 2015, http://www.unicefusa.org/mission/protect/trafficking.

Chapter 8 Two Gifts, One Package

1. "Netherlands," Global Slavery Index 2014, accessed July 7, 2015, http://www.globalslaveryindex.org/country/netherlands/.

Chapter 9 Just Call

1. "Sex Trafficking," International Justice Mission, accessed June 2, 2015, https://ijm.org/casework/sex-trafficking.
2. "IJM Chennai: Families Now Free from Forced Labor in 'Deplorable' Rice Mill," International Justice Mission, April 12, 2012, http://www.ijm.org/news/ijm-chennai-families-now-free-forced-labor-deplorable-rice-mill.

Chapter 10 Ice Cream and Insults

1. "What We Do," Restore International, accessed June 2, 2015, http://restoreinternational.org/what-we-do/.
2. C. S. Lewis, *Letters of C. S. Lewis* (Boston: Houghton Mifflin, 2003), 477.

Chapter 11 A Weekend in Pennsylvania

1. "Know It When You See It," Love146, accessed June 2, 2015, http://love146.org/report/.
2. Ewen Callaway, "Justice May Be Hard-Wired into the Human Brain," *New Scientist*, December 11, 2008, http://www.newscientist.com/article/dn16256-justice-may-be-hardwired-into-the-human-brain.html.

Chapter 12 Hide-and-Seek

1. Siddharth Kara, "Bonded Labor: Tackling the System of Slavery in South Asia" (New York: Columbia University Press, 2014), 202.

Chapter 13 A Teenage Stage Prop

1. "Human Trafficking," the A21 Campaign, accessed June 2, 2015, http://www.a21.org/content/human-trafficking/gl0ryw.
2. "Artisan Training Provides New Opportunities in Peruvian Amazon," Not For Sale, June 7, 2012, https://notforsalecampaign.org/stories/2012/06/07/artisan-training-provides-new-opportunities-in-peruvian-amazon/.

Chapter 14 Halfway There

1. US Department of State, *Trafficking in Persons Report June 2014*, "Introductory Material," 53, accessed June 17, 2015, http://www.state.gov/documents/organization/226844.pdf.

2. Robert Isaac Wilberforce, *The Life of William Wilberforce by His Sons, 4* (London: John Murray, 1838), 290, https://books.google.com/books?id=0i7dE45d1ZQC&printsec=frontcover&source=gbs_ge_summary_r&cad=0#v=onepage&q&f=false.

Chapter 15 Running on Adrenaline

1. US Department of State, *Trafficking in Persons Report June 2014*, "Introductory Material," 17, accessed July 16, 2015, http://www.state.gov/documents/organization/226844.pdf.

2. "IJM Manila, National Bureau of Investigation Bring 'Freedom and a New Life,'" International Justice Mission, July 18, 2012, https://www.ijm.org/news/ijm-manila-national-bureau-investigation-bring-freedom-and-new-life.

Chapter 16 Good Enough?

1. "Child Abuse Facts," Compassion International, accessed June 2, 2015, http://www.compassion.com/poverty/child-abuse.htm.

2. Louie Giglio, Twitter post, March 5, 2012, 7:51 a.m., http://twitter.com/louiegiglio.

Chapter 17 An Unexpected Gift

1. "Child Abuse Facts," Compassion International, accessed June 2, 2015, http://www.compassion.com/poverty/child-abuse.htm.

2. "Financial Training Begins in India," Not For Sale, December 11, 2012, http://notforsalecampaign.org/stories/2012/12/11/financial-training-begins-in-india/.

Chapter 18 The Day I Dyed

1. "Findings," Global Slavery Index 2014, accessed July 7, 2015, http://www.globalslaveryindex.org/findings/.

2. "Where We Work: Uganda," International Justice Mission, accessed July 7, 2015, https://www.ijm.org/where-we-work/uganda.

Chapter 19 Denim, Diamonds, and Desserts

1. "Our Solution," International Justice Mission, accessed June 2, 2015, https://ijm.org/our-solution.

Chapter 20 Hanging It Up

1. "Modern-Day Slavery," Not for Sale, accessed July 10, 2015, http://notforsalecampaign.org/human-trafficking/.

Bethany Winz is studying social justice at Trevecca Nazarene University where she's learning to love Nashville and urban farming. She already loves Jesus, hot tea, good books, and bacon. She processes the world by writing and blogs about the adventure of growing up and what she's learning about justice at www.bethanywinz.com. She grew up in Orlando, Florida, with her parents and her brother, and she sometimes misses living so close to her neighbor, Mickey Mouse.

Susanna Foth Aughtmon is the mother of three fantastic boys and the wife of Scott, the lead pastor of their church plant, Pathway Church, in Redwood City, California. She is the author of several books, including *All I Need Is Jesus and a Good Pair of Jeans: The Tired Supergirl's Search for Grace*, and a speaker with a heart for showing how God's grace and truth intersect with the reality of everyday living. She loves connecting with her readers through her speaking events and her blog, www.tiredsupergirl.com.

- Share or mention the book on your social media platforms. Use the hashtag **#onedressoneyear**.
- Write a book review on your blog or on a retailer site.
- Pick up a copy for friends, family, or strangers! Anyone who you think would enjoy and be challenged by its message.
- Share this message on Twitter or Facebook. **"I loved #OneDressOneYear by @BethanyWinz // BethanyWinz.com @ReadBakerBooks"**
- Recommend this book for your church, workplace, book club, or class.
- Follow Baker Books on social media and tell us what you like.